SPECTRUM® READING

Grade 8

CREDITS
Editor: Jennifer Stith
Cover Design: J.J. Giddings, Nick Pearson, Lynne Schwaner
Interior Design: Lyndsey Herring
Illustrations: J.J. Giddings, Max Porter

Spectrum®
An imprint of Carson Dellosa Education
PO Box 35665
Greensboro, NC 27425 USA

© 2025 Carson Dellosa Education. Except as permitted under the United States Copyright Act, no part of this publication may be reproduced, stored, or distributed in any form or by any means (mechanically, electronically, recording, etc.) without the prior written consent of Carson Dellosa Education. Spectrum® is an imprint of Carson Dellosa Education.

Printed in the USA • All rights reserved.
ISBN 978-1-4838-7480-7
01-1122512735

Table of Contents Grade 8

Introduction 4

Glossary of Terms 6

Chapter 1: Women in History 8

    Stanton and Anthony 10

    Ella Fitzgerald 14

    Eleanor Roosevelt 18

    Queen Liliuokalani 20

Chapter 2: Ordinary Kids, Extraordinary Deeds 24

    Kid of the Year 26

    Spread Kindness Like Wildflowers 30

    Volunteering Is for Kids 34

Chapter 3: Art & Illustration 36

    Who Is Banksy? 38

    Alma Thomas 42

    Anime for All Ages 46

    Finding a Way to the Comic Convention 50

    Born to Draw 54

Chapter 4: Fossils 58

    Stuck in the Pits 60

    Fossil Hunters 64

    Working with History 68

    Sue Hendrickson 72

    Coming Back to Life 76

    An Ancient Memento 80

Chapter 5: Search and Rescue 84

    Hidden Danger 86

    An Avalanche for Breakfast 90

Table of Contents Grade 8

    Canine Rescue 94

Chapter 6: Let's Eat! 98
    Julia Child 100
    Julia's Famous French Bread 104
    Garden Veggie Frittata 108
    An Experimental Appetite 112

Chapter 7: Space 116
    Planting a Seed for the Future 118
    Curiosity in Space 122
    Out of This World Experience 126
    Moon Veggies 130
    Home, Home on the Moon 134

Chapter 8: Under Water 138
    The Sturgeon General 140
    Fishing for Change 144
    Going the Distance 148
    Find a Way 152
    The Age of Aquarius 156
    Every Lap Counts 160
    The Ocean 164

Chapter 9: Bees 166
    Honey Hill Farm 168
    Sweet as Honey 172
    Summer of the Bees 176
    Morning Song of the Bees 180
    Brilliant Bees 182

Answer Key 186

Spectrum Introduction

For more than 20 years, Spectrum® workbooks have been the solution for helping students meet and exceed learning goals. Each title in the Spectrum workbook series offers grade-appropriate instruction and reinforcement for learning success.

Spectrum partners with you in supporting your student's educational journey every step of the way! This book will help them navigate eighth-grade reading and will give you the support you need to make sure your student learns everything they need to know. Inside you will find:

Chapter Introductions

These introductions provide useful information about the chapter, including:

- **Before-Reading Activities**
  These activities help students access background knowledge and set the stage for reading each section topic.

- **Helpful Definitions**
  These definitions, arranged in order of appearance in the chapter, help make unfamiliar words easier to understand.

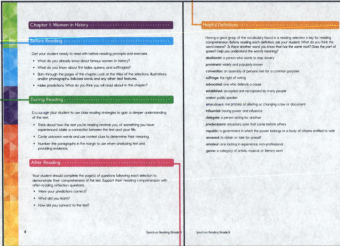

- **During-Reading Activities**
  These close-reading strategies help your student read for meaning and understanding.

- **After-Reading Activities**
  These activities give your student an opportunity to express what they have learned from the selection.

Reading Selections

These fiction and nonfiction reading selections cover multiple genres, including fictional stories, realistic fiction, informational text, poetry, and much more. The selections are followed by a series of questions designed to gauge student comprehension.

Selection Prompts

These sentences introduce each reading selection and give your student a quick idea of what they will be reading about in the selection.

Enrichment

These bonus problems appear throughout the book. They allow your student to dig deeper into the story or topic presented. The two types of problems encourage your student to extend their thinking  or explain and defend a concept .

Engaging Online Practice

Bring learning to life with fun, interactive activities on IXL! Look for the Skill ID and type the 3-digit code into the search bar on IXL.com or the IXL mobile app. Ten questions per day are free!

IXL.com skill ID **7K2**

Spectrum Reading **Grade 8**

Glossary of Terms

analogy: a comparison of things that are alike in some way; Example: *leaf is to tree as petal is to flower*

antagonist: a character who opposes another

author's purpose: the reason the author writes a text; can be to entertain, inform, or persuade

autobiography: a book in which the author tells the story of his or her life; Examples: *I Am Malala, Red Scarf Girl, Soul Surfer*

biography: a book that tells the life story of someone other than the author; Examples: *Black Women in Science, Amelia Lost*

characteristic: a typical feature or quality

cite: to quote from a written work

climax: the most exciting or important part of a story or an event, usually happening near the end

conflict: a clash or disagreement between opposing forces

evidence: information and facts that help prove something is true or not true

fantasy: a story with magical or strange characters, places, or events; Examples: *The Lightning Thief, Artemis Fowl*

fiction: stories about characters and events that are not real; Examples: *Bridge to Terabithia, Hatchet*

first-person point of view: the person telling the story is a character in the story; the reader knows what the person is thinking and feeling

historical fiction: stories in which the plot is inspired by a real-life event in the past, but the characters are fictional; Examples: *Heroes, Esperanza Rising, Number the Stars*

historical nonfiction: stories about real-life events and people; Examples: *Hidden Figures, The Finest Hours, No Better Friend*

hypothesis: an idea that could explain how something works but that has to be tested through experiments to be proven right

idiom: a commonly used expression whose meaning is not obvious, or not what you would expect; Example: *ants in your pants* means "extremely restless"

infographic: a visual representation of information or data; Examples: chart, graph, map, diagram

legend: a story handed down from earlier times, often based on fact but not entirely true; Examples: "Atlantis," "Pandora's Box," "The Wooden Horse of Troy"

main idea: the most important point or message the author wants to share in their writing

metaphor: a figure of speech that compares two things without using the words *like* or *as*; Examples: I am *an early bird*, so I was ready to go before my family was awake. The world *is a playground*. It's *raining cats and dogs*.

narrator: a person who tells a story

nonfiction: writing about real things, people, and events

personification: to give human qualities to animals or objects; Example: The fire *raged* throughout the night.

prefix: a word part added to the beginning of a word or root to change the meaning; Examples: *sub-*, *un-*, *dis-*

problem: a difficult situation that needs to be solved in a story

protagonist: the main character in a story

resolution: an answer; a solution

root (word): the most basic form of a word, is not a word on its own, needs a prefix and/or suffix added to it; Examples: *amb*iguous, *circum*ference, pro*ject*ion

second-person point of view: the person telling the story uses the pronoun *you* to address the reader, implying the reader is the main character

setting: the time and place where a story takes place

simile: a figure of speech that compares two things using the words *like* or *as*; Example: My mom was *as mad as a hornet* after someone scratched her car.

solution: the way a character in a story solves a problem

statement: something expressed in words

summary: a brief statement that gives the main points or ideas of something that has been written

theme: the main subject or idea of a piece of writing

third-person point of view: the person telling the story is not a character in the story; they are an outsider to the story

Chapter 1: Women in History

Before Reading

Get your student ready to read with before-reading prompts and exercises.

- What do you already know about famous women in history?
- What do you know about first ladies, queens, and suffragists?
- Skim through the pages of this chapter. Look at the titles of the selections, illustrations and/or photographs, italicized words, and any other text features.
- Make predictions. What do you think you will read about in this chapter?

During Reading

Encourage your student to use close-reading strategies to gain a deeper understanding of the text.

- Think about how the text you're reading reminds you of something you have experienced. Make a connection between the text and your life.
- Circle unknown words and use context clues to determine their meaning.
- Number the paragraphs in the margin to use when analyzing text and providing evidence.

After Reading

Your student should complete the page(s) of questions following each selection to demonstrate their comprehension of the text. Support their reading comprehension with after-reading reflection questions.

- Were your predictions correct?
- What did you learn?
- How did you connect to the text?

Helpful Definitions

Having a good grasp of the vocabulary found in a reading selection is key for reading comprehension. Before reading each definition, ask your student: *What do you think this word means? Is there another word you know that has the same root? Does the part of speech help you understand the word's meaning?*

abolitionist: a person who wants to stop slavery

prominent: widely and popularly known

convention: an assembly of persons who met for a common purpose

suffrage: the right to vote

advocated: one who defended a cause

established: accepted and recognized by many people

orator: public speaker

amendment: an altered or changed law or document

influential: having power and influence

delegate: a person acting for another

predecessors: ancestors; ones who come before others

republic: a government in which the power belongs to a body of citizens entitled to vote

coup: exercise of force

abdicated: renounced a throne or position

treaty: an agreement made by negotiation

annexed: obtained or taken for oneself

amateur: one lacking in experience; nonprofessional

genre: a category of artistic, musical, or literary work

Name _____

Chapter 1: Women in History

> What dynamic duo worked together to improve women's rights?

Stanton and Anthony

Elizabeth Cady Stanton was an activist, a writer, an editor, and an abolitionist. Born to a prominent couple in Johnstown, New York, she was well-educated and gained an understanding of law by spending time around the colleagues and guests of her father, who was a lawyer and state assemblyman. Elizabeth married Henry Stanton, an abolitionist lecturer. Elizabeth, too, became active in the anti-slavery movement and worked with other leading abolitionists.

For their honeymoon, Elizabeth and Henry traveled to the World Anti-Slavery Convention in London, England. While there, she was angered to find out that women were not recognized at the convention. She met Lucretia Mott, who was also angry about women being left out of the convention. They decided to call a women's convention to address the unfair treatment and improve women's rights.

The convention was held in Seneca Falls, New York. It helped start the equal rights movement for women. Stanton wrote "The Declaration of Sentiments," which added *woman* or *women* throughout the Declaration of Independence. The document outlined women's issues, such as the lack of the right to vote, to own property, receive equal wages, and many more.

Elizabeth Cady Stanton

Stanton made the women's suffrage movement, a campaign to secure women's right to vote, her top priority. Stanton met and later developed a working relationship with Susan B. Anthony. The two made a great team who dominated the women's rights movement for more than 50 years. Stanton could not travel much because she was raising her seven children. So, Stanton wrote the speeches, and Anthony delivered them to the public. They advocated for the 13th amendment, which ended slavery.

Chapter 1: Women in History

The pair established the National Woman Suffrage Association. Stanton became its president. She began traveling more after the Civil War, delivering speeches on topics of maternity, divorce law, property rights, and abolition. Stanton was a remarkable orator. However, Anthony was always the better known of the pair.

Anthony's travels across the country made her familiar to many Americans. She devoted all of her efforts to winning women's suffrage. Anthony called the first suffrage convention in Washington, DC. They proposed in Congress the first women's suffrage amendment.

Susan B. Anthony

After the Civil War, Anthony urged women to register to vote claiming the rights under the 14th and 15th amendments. Anthony and other women forced their way into voting lines and cast their ballots. She made headlines when she was arrested for voting. She used the trial and the newspaper coverage to gain support for her cause.

Meanwhile, Stanton continued to focus on improving educational opportunities for women. Together with Anthony, she published many volumes on the women's suffrage movement. Her autobiography, *Eighty Years and More*, was a huge success. Stanton continued to write about women's freedom and progress until her death in 1902, 18 years before women gained the right to vote.

Anthony devoted the rest of her life to winning the right to vote. She died in 1906, unable to see the 19th amendment pass in 1920. The amendment is known as the *Susan B. Anthony Amendment* as a tribute to her determination.

Name _____

Chapter 1: Women in History

> Answer the questions about *Stanton and Anthony*.

1. What prompted Elizabeth Cady Stanton to organize a convention in Seneca Falls, New York?

   _____
   _____
   _____

2. Why was Susan B. Anthony more well known than Elizabeth Cady Stanton?

   _____ Anthony traveled more and saw more of the public.

   _____ Anthony made the speeches.

   _____ Stanton was the speechwriter and remained in the background much of the time.

   _____ all of the above

3. Use evidence from the text to best pinpoint the time period for the selection.

   _____
   _____
   _____

4. In your own words, describe what an abolitionist was.

   _____
   _____

Name _____

Chapter 1: Women in History

Search for this skill ID on IXL.com for more practice!

IXL.com skill ID
7K2

5. What is the author's opinion of Stanton and Anthony? Cite evidence from the text to support your answer.

_____

_____

_____

_____

6. Conduct further research about the Seneca Falls Convention. How does it relate to the following movements?

Abolition	
Civil Rights	
Suffrage	

Spectrum Reading Grade 8

13

Chapter 1: Women in History

> Read all about the "First Lady of Song."

Ella Fitzgerald

When 16-year-old Ella Fitzgerald took the stage at Harlem's Apollo Theater, she had no idea her life was about to change.

Fitzgerald's childhood had been hard. Her parents divorced shortly after her birth, and her father left her and her mother. Then, when she was a teenager, her mother passed away. After the death of her mother, Fitzgerald struggled to find herself. She was sent to reform school, but she was treated poorly there and escaped.

Fitzgerald found herself broke and alone during the Great Depression. She kept the memories of her parents alive through her love of music, which she shared with them. She took piano lessons, sang, and danced. She used this musical knowledge to perform on the streets of Harlem to make some money.

Name _____

Chapter 1: Women in History

On the memorable night Fitzgerald's life would change in 1934, she planned to dance during amateur night at the Apollo. But when she saw the other dancers perform, she panicked. She didn't think her performance would live up to the dancers who went before her. What she ended up doing instead was singing her mother's favorite song. The audience was enthralled and cheered for an encore. She won first place.

A band director was in the audience when she won, and he saw her talent. He got her an audition with a famous bandleader. At home, Fitzgerald was shy and reserved, but onstage, she felt fearless. Fitzgerald was a success at the audition, and she joined the band. Through the band, she was introduced to others in the jazz world, and her career took off.

In 1936, Fitzgerald recorded her first single, "Love and Kisses." In 1938, she recorded her first hit, "A-Tisket, A-Tasket." It was on the top of the music charts for 17 weeks. She went on tour with a popular jazz band and performed across the United States and then the world. She became an international star.

Fitzgerald's musical career spanned six decades. During that time, she released more than 200 albums. She won 13 Grammy Awards. She received her last Grammy in 1990. Fitzgerald worked with some of the greatest American singers of the twentieth century, including Frank Sinatra, Louis Armstrong, Count Basie, and Dizzy Gillespie. Her talent and charm pleased a wide range of listeners around the world and helped make jazz a more popular genre.

Fitzgerald never took her success for granted. She gave money to charities that cared for needy children. In 1992, she received the Presidential Medal of Freedom, one of the highest honors available to civilians. Ella Fitzgerald gave her final performance in New York's Carnegie Hall. She died in 1996. However, the American "First Lady of Song" continues to live in the hearts of music lovers worldwide.

Name _____

Chapter 1: Women in History

Answer the questions about *Ella Fitzgerald*.

1. Which of the following best defines the word *renowned*?

   wealthy

   talented

   famous

   underappreciated

2. Why did the author include, *At home, Fitzgerald was shy and reserved, but onstage, she felt fearless?*

   _____
   _____
   _____
   _____

3. Number the following events in the order in which they happened.

   _____ Fitzgerald won a contest to perform during amateur night at the Apollo Theater in New York City.

   _____ Fitzgerald received the Presidential Medal of Freedom.

   _____ Fitzgerald gave her final performance.

   _____ Fitzgerald received her final Grammy Award.

Name _____

Chapter 1: Women in History

4. How did Fitzgerald help make jazz a more popular musical genre? Use evidence from the text to support your answer.

_____
_____
_____
_____

5. Why do you think Ella Fitzgerald is called the "First Lady of Song"?

_____
_____
_____

Have you ever felt confident doing something you love to do? Explain.

_____
_____
_____
_____
_____
_____

Chapter 1: Women in History

> Who overcame shyness and became one of the most influential first ladies?

Eleanor Roosevelt

Eleanor Roosevelt is often described as one of the most influential first ladies in American history. However, as a child, Eleanor Roosevelt was lonely and shy. Unfortunately, she lost both parents during her childhood. After their deaths, she was raised by her grandmother.

As a teenager, Eleanor Roosevelt attended a boarding school in England. There, she met a teacher who helped her gain self-confidence. When she returned to the United States, she began her career as a human rights activist. In 1905, Eleanor married Franklin Delano Roosevelt. Franklin was an intelligent, young politician. Together, they raised five children.

In 1921, Franklin caught polio. Eleanor became his political eyes and ears. She visited people all over the nation. She learned about their problems and reported them to her husband. She also became active in political groups. She was a member of the women's division of the New York State Democratic Committee.

Franklin Delano Roosevelt became president in 1933. Eleanor changed the role of the first lady. She was the first first lady to hold regular press conferences. She also allowed only female reporters, providing opportunities to journalists who were often denied access to the White House. She also traveled, lectured, spoke on the radio, and wrote a daily newspaper column. Eleanor also worked to improve the lives of needy people. She fought for women's rights and supported the civil rights movement. After President Roosevelt's death, Eleanor became an American delegate to the United Nations. She had come a long way from the shy girl she used to be.

Name _____

Chapter 1: Women in History

Answer the questions about *Eleanor Roosevelt.*

1. Underline the word in the text that means *the people who previously held a particular job.*

2. Write four ways in which Eleanor changed the role of first lady.

   _____
   _____
   _____
   _____

3. Eleanor became *the political eyes and ears* of Franklin Delano Roosevelt. What does that phrase mean?

   _____
   _____
   _____
   _____

4. What type of text is this selection an example of? Explain the characteristics that make it this type of text.

   _____
   _____
   _____
   _____

Spectrum Reading Grade 8

Name _____

Chapter 1: Women in History

> Did you know that Hawaii was once ruled by a queen?

Queen Liliuokalani

Before Hawaii was a state, it was a kingdom. When Lydia Kamaka'eha's brother was crowned king of Hawaii in 1874, she didn't know she would soon be named Queen Liliuokalani's (li-lee-uh-wo-kuh-la-nee). She also didn't know she would be the last ruling monarch the kingdom would ever have.

Growing up in a royal family, Liliuokalani received an excellent education. She learned English by age four and traveled around the world as a young girl. In 1881, her brother, King Kalakaua, left on a long trip and put Liliuokalani in charge of Hawaii while he was gone.

Name _____

Chapter 1: Women in History

    Then, disaster struck in Hawaii. A terrible disease, smallpox, arrived. Liliuokalani acted quickly. She discovered that the sickness was being brought into Hawaii, so she closed the ports. This made Americans who shipped sugar from the Hawaiian Islands very angry. But, Liliuokalani cared about her people and their ability to get well.

    Liliuokalani's brother, King Kalakaua, died in 1891. Liliuokalani became the first woman to ever ascend the throne of the Hawaiian kingdom. By the time she had become queen, the United States had gained a lot of power in Hawaii. Queen Liliuokalani wanted to change American laws that took away her power as queen. She wanted to use that power to take care of her people and give them more rights.

    Liliuokalani started making changes to take back the power of the Hawaiian monarchy. But this was not a welcome change for foreign businesspeople, whose ability to make money depended on the agreements they had made with prior kings. They arranged a coup and Liliuokalani surrendered and abdicated the throne so that no one would get hurt. A treaty stating that Hawaii would give up power and agree to be governed by the United States was created.

    Liliuokalani wrote to President Grover Cleveland, asking him to reinstate her as queen. Cleveland listened to her and ordered for her to be restored to her throne. But those who had led the coup in Hawaii didn't listen. They kept Liliuokalani under house arrest and jailed her supporters until she agreed to sign a formal abdication.

    In 1898, Hawaii was officially annexed, or added, to the United States. Liliuokalani lived the rest of her life in Hawaii, always fighting for native Hawaiians to have power over their land. She wrote an autobiography *Hawaii's Story by Hawaii's Queen* and a song "Aloha Oe," which is still loved today. In 1959, Hawaii achieved statehood. Today, Hawaiians remember Queen Liliuokalani for her strong leadership.

Spectrum Reading Grade 8

Name _____

Chapter 1: Women in History

Answer the questions about *Queen Liliuokalani*.

1. Which of the following is another good title for the passage? Explain your choice.

    A Queen in Prison   *Hawaii*

    The Last Queen of Hawaii   *A New State*

    _____

    _____

    _____

2. Use the text to define the word *republic*.

    _____

    _____

3. Number the events in the order in which they happened.

    _____ Hawaiians remember Queen Liliuokalani for her strong leadership.

    _____ Liliuokalani became queen.

    _____ Hawaii became a republic.

    _____ Liliuokalani closed Hawaii's ports to protect the people from smallpox.

    _____ Liliuokalani's brother left her in charge of Hawaii while he was traveling.

Name _____

Chapter 1: Women in History

4. Do you think all Americans were in favor of Hawaii being annexed? Why or why not?

_____
_____
_____

5. What kind of queen was Liliuokalani? How do you know?

_____
_____
_____

When did the state in which you live become a state? Conduct research and write what you learn below.

_____
_____
_____
_____
_____
_____

Chapter 2: Ordinary Kids, Extraordinary Deeds

Before Reading

Get your student ready to read with before-reading prompts and exercises.

- What special skills do you have?
- What causes do you feel strongly about?
- Skim through the pages of this chapter. Look at the titles of the selections, illustrations and/or photographs, italicized words, and any other text features.
- Make predictions. What do you think you will read about in this chapter?

During Reading

Encourage your student to use close-reading strategies to gain a deeper understanding of the text.

- Visualize what is happening in the reading selection while you are reading it. If it is fiction, create the characters and setting in your mind and watch the story play out as you read it. If it is nonfiction, call upon your knowledge of the topic to visualize things that are mentioned in the selection.
- Create a timeline of events from a fictional story.
- Ask yourself what the theme or main idea of the selection is.

After Reading

Your student should complete the page(s) of questions following each selection to demonstrate their comprehension of the text. Support their reading comprehension with after-reading reflection questions.

- Were your predictions correct?
- What did you learn?
- How did you connect to the text?

Helpful Definitions

Having a good grasp of the vocabulary found in a reading selection is key for reading comprehension. Before reading each definition, ask your student: *What do you think this word means? Is there another word you know that has the same root? Does the part of speech help you understand the word's meaning?*

cyberbullying: bullying done on the Internet

contaminated: containing harmful or undesirable substances

innovation: a new idea or invention

initiative: the ability to take action without being told to do so

influence: the power to cause an effect

ambassador: the top person sent by a government to represent a country

empowering: giving someone power, authority, or ability they did not have before

résumé: a brief list or summary of a person's education, jobs, and achievements

obstacle: something that gets in the way of progress

Name _____

Chapter 2: Ordinary Kids, Extraordinary Deeds

How does a 15-year-old stop cyberbullying?

Kid of the Year

Kids can make a difference in the world at any age. If you don't believe it, check out the cover of *Time* magazine for December 14, 2020. Beside a full-page photo of a young woman in a lab coat, the cover headline reads: "KID of the YEAR: SCIENTIST AND INVENTOR, Gitanjali Rao, 15."

So, how did a 15-year-old kid make the cover of one of the most popular magazines in the country and get interviewed by the famous actor, Angelina Jolie?

Gitanjali was one of five finalists chosen from more than 5,000 kids, ages eight to 16, for making an impact on the world. She was *Time*'s first-ever Kid of the Year because of her outstanding work using technology to solve problems such as contaminated drinking water, cyberbullying, and opioid addiction—just for starters.

Her talent for finding tech solutions for everyday problems was first noticed in a big way when she was in seventh grade. Gitanjali won the 2017 Discovery Education 3M Young Scientist Challenge for an inexpensive and portable device that tests for lead in drinking water. Combine this with her smartphone app to analyze the results and watch her win a $25,000 prize! Cities around the world now had a way to easily test their water systems.

Fame and fortune did not stop Gitanjali. She continued to use technology to create more change in the world, in a good way. One of her more recent inventions is called Kindly. It's a phone app she created with a Chrome extension. It is programed to pick up cyberbullying by pointing out specific words or phrases. If a kid is texting someone, they may not even realize they're using bullying words, especially if they're angry. She tried it out with other teens, and they liked and understood the goal.

Gitanjali knows she can't do it all herself, so she works to get other teens engaged in solving the world's problems—more than 30,000 at last count. She partners with rural schools, other girls in local STEM organizations, as well as museums around the world. She runs what she calls innovation workshops for large, global institutions that involve kids in science, technology, and engineering.

Name _____

Chapter 2: Ordinary Kids, Extraordinary Deeds

Gitanjali teaches her process to the kids in her workshops. It's simple: "observe, brainstorm, research, build, communicate." At the end of each session, she wants the students to go home with a project to start working on—something to make the world a better place for someone.

She gets excited when she hears back from one of her workshop students. "Hey, I attended your workshop four months ago and here's my finished product, I really love it, it's a shoe that calls 911."

Gitanjali stresses that no one need think they should or could fix everything that's wrong with the world. She encourages students to start with something small and go from there. "Even if it's something as small as, *I want to find an easy way to pick up litter.*"

So, what's next for Gitanjali? In 2024, she was a freshman at the Massachusetts Institute of Technology (MIT), a world-renowned research university. She has big plans for the future of the world and herself.

"Hi, I'm Gitanjali," she says on her website. "It's nice to meet you. I'm 18 years old and a freshman at MIT, Cambridge. My goal is to create global change by starting an innovation movement of teens looking to make a difference."

Let's celebrate and join the world of teens who care. Are you in?

Spectrum Reading **Grade 8**

Name _____

Chapter 2: Ordinary Kids, Extraordinary Deeds

Answer the questions about *Kid of the Year*.

1. List the problems mentioned in the text that Gitanjali solved with technology.

   _____
   _____
   _____
   _____

2. What are the steps of Gitanjali's process for solving problems?

   _____
   _____
   _____
   _____

3. Gitanjali states that her goal is to "create global change by starting an innovation movement of teens looking to make a difference." Explain in your own words what she means.

   _____
   _____
   _____
   _____

Name _____

Chapter 2: Ordinary Kids, Extraordinary Deeds

4. Write one fact presented in the text.

   _____

   _____

5. Write one opinion presented in the text.

   _____

   _____

Create a timeline of Gitanjali's life and accomplishments. Do research to add two more events not included in the text.

Spectrum Reading Grade 8

Name _____

Chapter 2: Ordinary Kids, Extraordinary Deeds

How does one young man plan to spread kindness all over the world?

Spread Kindness Like Wildflowers

Orion Jean is a Haitian American young man on a mission. All he wants to do is spread kindness in the world.

"Hello, my name is Orion Jean," reads the opening statement on his website. "I am 13 years old and am in the eighth grade. I created my own initiative called the 'Race to Kindness' to help spread kindness all over the world."

Orion is on the move. He never stops thinking about other people. His work has gotten him a lot of attention. He's been a guest on *Ellen*, *Good Morning America*, and the *CBS Evening News*. Besides making headlines in numerous newspapers, Orion was selected in 2022 as *Time* magazine's 2021 Kid of the Year.

The spotlight first shone on him in 2020 when he wrote a speech about kindness. He entered it into a student kindness contest and won! He used the money to spread his message . . . and kindness.

First, Orion started collecting toys, which he donated to the Dallas Children's Hospital. The nurses told him it was the largest donation they'd received there, and that it would make a lot of kids happy. Bingo! That was all Orion wanted, and he treasures the memory.

He has also found ways to donate more than 100,000 meals to hungry families in his home state of Texas. He accomplished this by holding food drives and working with a local relief group.

Orion's many acts of kindness have earned him the title of Kindness Ambassador. Let's look at his love of books. Orion wants to share the joy of reading with everyone.

"I want to be able to share my love of literacy with as many people as possible," he told his interviewer on the *CBS Evening News* program. Orion walks his talk. To date, he's donated over 500,000 books.

He's also published books—his own! When Orion was a 10-year-old fifth grader, he wrote a book called *A Kids Book About Leadership™*. He believes everyone can be a leader, no matter their age.

Name _____

Chapter 2: Ordinary Kids, Extraordinary Deeds

"Your ideas and your thoughts matter," he says in the book. "Even if you feel small you can influence just 1 person. And that 1 person can influence someone in their own lives, causing a ripple effect, which all together can change the world."

Orion has another book out, hot off the press in May 2024. *Race to Kindness* is a picture book for younger children, ages four to eight. He tells kids that the smallest act of kindness can make a big difference in someone else's life. His suggestions are simple, such as sharing a snack or giving a compliment. This book is also available on Amazon, with a 4.9-star rating. Kids can do amazing things!

Orion's mission didn't stop with publishing the book. He also is responsible for having donated more than half a million copies.

He's called his latest project the "Race to 1,000,000 Kindnesses." He is hoping that in one year, people will have chosen to be kind to another person one million times . . . or more.

"Anything is possible with the power of belief, the power of kindness," Orion said. "Choose to go out there and be kind."

Orion has a challenge to each and every one of us: "I believe that everyone can make a difference. I am committed to inspiring and empowering people of all ages to be kind to each other, no matter what. Join me in the "Race to Kindness . . . the best part is EVERYONE WINS."

Spectrum Reading Grade 8

Name _____

Chapter 2: Ordinary Kids, Extraordinary Deeds

Answer the questions about *Spread Kindness Like Wildflowers*.

1. Which sentence do you think best develops the main idea of the text? Explain.

   _____
   _____
   _____
   _____

2. What does Orion say can be a *rippling effect*?

   _____
   _____

3. The title is a simile. Explain why you think the author chose the title of this article.

   _____
   _____
   _____
   _____

4. Come up with an alternative title for the text.

   _____
   _____

Name _____

Chapter 2: Ordinary Kids, Extraordinary Deeds

5. What is one small act of kindness Orion says can make a big difference? Do you agree or disagree? Explain.

_____
_____
_____
_____
_____
_____

Considering Orion's previous acts, what could you predict about his future career?

_____
_____
_____
_____
_____
_____

Name _____

Chapter 2: Ordinary Kids, Extraordinary Deeds

How can you help in your community?

Volunteering Is for Kids

Volunteering

is a great way to help others—and get out of your own way. Start small. Think about something you're interested in, good at, or touched by. Do research. See what other kids your age are doing. Stop by your community volunteer center. Use the Internet to get information on groups and organizations that need help.

Your local animal shelter may allow you to regularly walk or pet their stray animals. You will probably need to go in with an adult.

Volunteer to help coach a local sports team for little kids. Or offer to give private lessons to a kid who is struggling to get up to bat.

If you play an instrument, find a budding musician whose family can't afford lessons and give them lessons—for free! Start a band!

Search out your local soup kitchen or a homeless shelter. You may be able to serve food or wash dishes.

Do you like to garden? There's probably a community garden in your area, growing vegetables or flowers to help people experiencing poverty. If not, start one!

34
Spectrum Reading Grade 8

Name _____

Chapter 2: Ordinary Kids, Extraordinary Deeds

Answer the questions about *Volunteering Is for Kids*.

1. What's a good way to start volunteering?

   _____
   _____
   _____

2. Write down some obstacles you might face.

   _____
   _____
   _____
   _____

 Share some volunteer ideas with a family member. Make an action plan with measurable goals.

_____
_____
_____
_____
_____
_____

Spectrum Reading **Grade 8**

Chapter 3: Art & Illustration

Before Reading

Get your student ready to read with before-reading prompts and exercises.

- Do you enjoy drawing or painting? In what style?
- Who are some artists and/or illustrators you know about?
- Skim through the pages of this chapter. Look at the titles of the selections, illustrations and/or photographs, italicized words, and any other text features.
- Make predictions. What do you think you will read about in this chapter?

During Reading

Encourage your student to use close-reading strategies to gain a deeper understanding of the text.

- Jot down questions that come up as you are reading.
- Read out loud. Read a passage slowly and listen to what you are saying as you are reading. Read to a friend, family member, your pet, or just out loud to yourself.
- Number the paragraphs in the margin to use when analyzing text and providing evidence.

After Reading

Your student should complete the page(s) of questions following each selection to demonstrate their comprehension of the text. Support their reading comprehension with after-reading reflection questions.

- Were your predictions correct?
- What did you learn?
- How did you connect to the text?

Helpful Definitions

Having a good grasp of the vocabulary found in a reading selection is key for reading comprehension. Before reading each definition, ask your student: *What do you think this word means? Is there another word you know that has the same root? Does the part of speech help you understand the word's meaning?*

anonymous: written, done, or given by a person whose name is not known or made public

influential: having the power to change or affect someone or something

ravine: a steep, extremely narrow valley

pediatric: of or relating to the care of babies and children

commemorate: to honor and remember an important person or event

demeanor: the way you behave

replica: an exact copy of something, especially a copy made on a smaller scale than the original

submission: acceptance of or giving in to the will or authority of someone or something

radical: thorough and has wide range of important effects

anime: Japanese animation for film, television, and video

manga: a kind of Japanese comic that often has stories with a science fiction theme

exaggerated: made something seem bigger, better, more important, or more extreme than it really is

flawed: having a defect

convention: a formal gathering of people who have the same profession or interests

waned: became less important

aspirations: desires for future achievements

reimburse: to pay back money spent on your behalf

intentions: what someone has in mind in terms of goals or purpose

Name _____

Chapter 3: Art & Illustration

> Who is the artist who has yet to be identified?

Who Is Banksy?

The art of one of the most famous living artists today is known around the world. You'd know his work if you saw it, especially since it's usually on a wall. Who is this artist? Well . . . no one knows his name!

This anonymous street artist goes by the name of Banksy. He paints on large outdoor surfaces such as buildings, trains, streets, and bridges. He uses spray paints, mostly, and creates his images with stencils he has made. Yes, Banksy is a graffiti artist. And yes, spray painting graffiti on public spaces is illegal. Do *not* be like Banksy.

For someone without a known name, Banksy has earned quite a name for himself. In 2010, he made *Time* magazine's list of most influential people, along with President Obama, Elon Musk, and Lady Gaga. He is that famous. But no one even knows what he looks like. For the article, instead of a head shot, he sent in a photo of himself with a paper bag over his head.

If anyone knows his real name, they aren't saying. We know he is a man, he grew up in England, and his hometown is probably Bristol. We think he was born in 1974. We think he is married. His last name might be Banks.

This mysterious artist started painting when he was 14. He was an unhappy student and was eventually expelled from school. He landed in prison for a time. But he had things to say, made graffiti his voice, and continued to speak out against the wrongs in the world, such as war and poverty.

Banksy's most famous painting, *Girl with Balloon*, was part of a London street art series he painted under a bridge starting in 2002. It is a simple illustration of a little girl in black and white who is reaching for a red, heart-shaped balloon.

Her hand is just inches away from the string of the balloon. Beside it, Banksy painted the words: THERE IS ALWAYS HOPE. No one knows if the balloon has just slipped out of her hand or if she is about to catch it.

The floating balloon painting was destroyed long ago, but Banksy printed limited edition prints of it. Banksy fans went wild for these prints, which are now quite valuable.

Chapter 3: Art & Illustration

In fact, one of them sold at auction for more than $1 million in 2018. As the gavel went down, the buyer began to rejoice that Banksy's most famous image was now hers. But within minutes, half of the piece was cut into paper ribbons by a shredder Banksy had hidden in the frame. Banksy strikes again!

The buyer of the shredded Banksy print said she would still pay for it. "I was at first shocked," she said, "but gradually I began to realize that I would end up with my own piece of art history." The print has been renamed, *Love Is in the Bin*. (In England, a *bin* is a trash or garbage can.)

Banksy has painted pictures on towers, bridges, water towers, and even mobile homes in countries around the world. Three years after Hurricane Katrina hit New Orleans, Louisiana, Banksy stenciled his artwork on abandoned buildings there. A mobile home in England, which he spray-painted a 30-foot mural on, sold for $500,000. The couple who owned it had paid only $1,000 for it 11 years earlier.

Banksy continues to paint, usually as a form of protest. He painted a few works of art on abandoned buildings in the Gaza Strip and posted them on his website. During the pandemic, he donated a painting to a hospital so the proceeds could go to help the sick. He has created graffiti murals on war-damaged walls in Ukraine.

Banksy has given next to no interviews. Most of what we know about his thoughts and opinions comes from his website. "As a kid, I always dreamt of growing up to be a character in *Robin Hood*," he wrote. "I just never realized I'd end up playing one of the gold coins."

Spectrum Reading Grade 8

Name _____

Chapter 3: Art & Illustration

Answer the questions about *Who Is Banksy?*

1. How would you describe the artist Banksy?

   _____
   _____
   _____
   _____

2. What are some places where Banksy has created his art?

   _____
   _____
   _____
   _____

3. Restate in your own words what happened to the piece of art that sold at auction.

   _____
   _____
   _____
   _____
   _____
   _____

Name _____

Chapter 3: Art & Illustration

4. What conclusions can you draw about why this happened?

   _____
   _____
   _____
   _____
   _____

Do you agree with Banksy's desire to remain anonymous? Give at least three reasons to support your answer.

_____
_____
_____
_____
_____
_____
_____

Chapter 3: Art & Illustration

> What artist defined their signature style at the age of 75?

Alma Thomas

Alma Thomas was born in 1891, the oldest of four girls. Facing racial violence in their area of Georgia, her family moved north to Washington, DC. Although DC was segregated, more opportunities were available to African Americans than in most cities of that time.

While growing up, her family supported and emphasized learning and culture. Thomas attended Howard University and became the university's first fine arts graduate. After graduating, Thomas began a 35-year career teaching art at a junior high school. Thomas was devoted to her students, organizing clubs and exhibitions for them. Teaching art allowed Thomas to support herself while pursuing her own painting.

Chapter 3: Art & Illustration

Thomas also earned a master's in arts education at Columbia University and studied art at American University. She experimented with different styles, drawing from the great painters who came before her. It was not until she retired from teaching that she honed her style. At age 75, Thomas debuted several pieces of her artwork at Howard University.

Thomas experimented with abstraction. Her colorful and rhythmically patterned works were inspired by nature. Washington, DC's parks, her own garden, and memories of her childhood home were all inspirations. Thomas often said that through color, she could paint beauty and happiness. She did not want to focus on the mistreatment of other humans during that time.

In 1972, Thomas was the first Black woman to have a solo exhibition at the Whitney Museum of American Art. She reflected on this event and her segregated childhood saying, "One of the things we couldn't do was go into museums, let alone think of hanging our pictures there. My, times have changed. Just look at me now." Thomas became an important role model for older artists, women, and African Americans.

Name _____

Chapter 3: Art & Illustration

Answer the questions about *Alma Thomas*.

1. Why did the author include the text, *her family supported and emphasized learning and culture?*

   _____
   _____
   _____

2. Use the text to define the word *exhibition*.

   _____
   _____

3. Explain Thomas's attitude toward the times as mentioned in the last paragraph.

   _____
   _____
   _____
   _____

4. Thomas did not establish her true style of painting until after she retired. Explain why you think that's important to the text.

   _____
   _____
   _____
   _____

Name _____

Chapter 3: Art & Illustration

5. Name two of the author's purposes for writing this selection.

_____
_____
_____
_____

Research some of Thomas's works. Write an opinion paragraph on her works as they relate to the dark times of the civil rights era.

_____
_____
_____
_____
_____
_____
_____
_____
_____

Name _____

Chapter 3: Art & Illustration

> What are the characteristics of anime?

Anime for All Ages

Can adults enjoy cartoons as much as children do? Fans of anime would say, YES! Anime is a style of animation that originated in Japan. Its subject matter can be lighthearted and appropriate for children. But anime also covers more serious topics than typically used in the cartoons of Western culture. While some forms of anime are intended for children, there are also genres that appeal to adults.

Anime is rooted in Japan's past. Japan was an isolated country before it was opened to the Western world in the 1800s. Manga, or comic strips, had existed for many centuries. Japanese comic artists learned new techniques from their Western counterparts. They began to use word balloons in their manga and separated their stories into boxed sequences. These became incorporated into manga. Like Western comic artists, manga artists poked fun at authority and questioned the government. These comic strips appeared in newspapers, and their artists enjoyed great popularity.

During the 1920s and 1930s, the Japanese government began to pressure manga artists to stop drawing such comics. They did not want artists to raise questions about the country's leadership. This pressure increased in the early 1940s, during World War II. Suddenly, artists who had spent their careers criticizing the government were forced to praise it. These same artists began to draw cartoons that showed only positive aspects of life in Japan.

After Japan was defeated in World War II, there were many changes in Japanese life. Citizens enjoyed more freedom. Once again, there was much opportunity for manga artists. Some formed their own small publishing companies and began animating their works. Anime began to thrive.

Anime has a distinct style. Artists portray characters with huge eyes, small mouths, and pointy hairdos. In fact, many of these attributes were taken from the cartoons produced by Walt Disney during the 1940s and 1950s.

Name _____

Chapter 3: Art & Illustration

In anime, large eyes represent honesty and innocence. A sneaky character is drawn with smaller eyes. The smallest eyes are used to show that characters have an evil nature and cannot be trusted. Similarly, a sudden shift in the character's eye size is used to convey strong emotion. For example, when a kind character feels very angry, his or her eyes become very tiny. It is much more common for characters to be shown with "happy eyes," though. These eyes are dark half circles that dominate the face.

The color used for an anime character's hair can be very meaningful. Hair color tells the viewer about a character's personality. Red hair shows strong emotion, such as a strong or passionate spirit. A blue-haired character is typically calm and dependable. Western audiences might interpret these colors to be the character's actual hair color. To Japanese audiences, these colors merely describe a character's personality. It is generally assumed that all characters are dark-haired!

Eyes and hair are not the only unique qualities of anime. The character's body types are very exaggerated, as well as their expressions and gestures. Action scenes in anime are cut abruptly, so that actions end very suddenly. The angles that anime artists use to draw scenes are unusual. Scenes are often shown from perspectives very different than used in Western cartoons. When two characters are very angry, sparks might literally connect one to the other.

The approach to subject matter in anime also reflects Japanese culture and attitudes. Many anime series are based on young characters, as in Western cartoons. Whereas Western characters are typically heroic and confident, Japanese anime characters are flawed. They strive for perfection. This can be traced to the pressure to succeed in Japanese education. If you enjoy comics and animation, you may want to check out manga or anime. Compare it to the animation you're familiar with. Which do you like better?

Name _____

Chapter 3: Art & Illustration

Answer the questions about *Anime for All Ages.*

1. How do Japanese anime characters reflect Japanese culture?

   _____
   _____
   _____

2. How was manga different in the years leading up to World War II than it was in the years following the war?

   _____
   _____
   _____
   _____

3. The author's purpose in writing this selection was

   _____ to persuade the reader that Japanese animation is superior to Western animation.

   _____ to entertain the reader with humorous accounts of Japanese animation.

   _____ to inform the reader about Japanese anime and its history.

4. In paragraph 8, what does *exaggerated* mean?

   _____
   _____

Spectrum Reading Grade 8

Name _____

Chapter 3: Art & Illustration

5. What is the significance of hair color in anime?

   _____

   _____

   _____

6. Write **T** for true or **F** for false next to each statement below.

   _____ In anime, trustworthy characters are drawn with very small eyes.

   _____ Anime began years before manga did.

   _____ Japanese anime was influenced by the style of Walt Disney.

   _____ Anime is enjoyed by children and adults.

> Have you ever seen anime? If not, are you more likely to after reading this selection? Explain.
>
> _____
>
> _____
>
> _____
>
> _____
>
> _____

Spectrum Reading Grade 8

Name _____

Chapter 3: Art & Illustration

> Will Malik find a way to save enough money to make it to the comic convention?

Finding a Way to the Comic Convention

Malik sighed as he counted the last pieces of change that he had found hiding in his winter jacket. When Malik's dad had offered to let him go to the comic convention this year in San Diego, Malik could hardly believe his good luck. He had been pleading to go to the massive comic book convention for the past three years. The deal was that Mr. Goode would go with Malik if Malik could pay for his own airfare. Malik had some money saved from his previous birthday and from walking the dog that used to live across the street, but he had a bad habit of spending his weekly allowance before it ever got anywhere near his savings jar.

Malik threw himself onto his bed, feeling half defeated and half determined to figure out a way to get to the convention. A moment later, his bedroom door opened, and Shaun walked in, his nose buried in a book. Malik could never figure out how his little brother managed to walk that way without seriously injuring himself.

"Are you still moping about the convention?" asked Shaun.

Malik just nodded, knowing that his brother didn't understand his obsession with going to the convention. Shaun was enthusiastic about anything related to space and space travel. As far as Malik knew, his brother had never even opened a comic book.

Malik, on the other hand, had been a serious fan of graphic novels ever since he was in second grade. He had had difficulty learning to read fluently and had become discouraged by school and homework. Malik's mom had introduced him to graphic novels one day at the library, hoping they would capture his attention. Mrs. Goode had been exactly right, and Malik's love for all things animated had begun.

Six years later, reading was no longer an issue for Malik, but his interest in graphic novels had never waned. He wrote his own now and illustrated them in his spare time. He had aspirations of attending art school and someday having his own series of comics. He wanted to go to the comic convention to see the latest artwork by the illustrators he admired. Malik visited the convention's website often and knew that more than 130,000 visitors were expected this year. There would be film screenings, games, hands-on workshops, and a costume competition. He could probably get autographs for all five of his favorite graphic novels. Malik groaned at the mere thought of all he'd be missing and rolled over on his bed.

Chapter 3: Art & Illustration

"How much money are you short?" asked Shaun.

"One hundred and thirty-seven dollars," said Malik. "Dad said he'd pay for our hotel and food, but I need to come up with the money for the plane ticket."

"How many weeks are left before the convention?" asked Shaun, opening up the laptop that he and Malik shared.

"Nine," answered Malik without hesitation. The dates had been marked on his calendar ever since they were first announced.

"This is totally doable," responded Shaun enthusiastically. He made a quick spreadsheet and turned the screen so his brother could see it. "You just need to save your entire allowance. And if you do my chores for me for the next two months," added Shaun, "I'll give you half my allowance. As long as Dad will buy your ticket and let you reimburse him, you're good to go."

Malik shook his head in disbelief. "This is so simple," he admitted. "I feel a little sheepish that I didn't come up with this in the first place, Shaun. I owe you one. Let me know if there's an autograph or something I can bring back for you."

Shaun shook his head. "No autographs, thanks," he responded, "but I'm pretty sure there's a space center in San Diego that has some pretty cool souvenirs . . . ."

Spectrum Reading Grade 8

Name _____

Chapter 3: Art & Illustration

Answer the questions about *Finding a Way to the Comic Convention.*

1. Describe how Shaun and Malik are different from one another.

   _____
   _____
   _____

2. In paragraph 11, what does *reimburse* mean?

   _____
   _____

3. How would you characterize Malik and Shaun's relationship?

   _____
   _____
   _____

4. Do you think the deal that Mr. Goode proposes to Malik is fair? Why or why not?

   _____
   _____
   _____
   _____

Name _____

Chapter 3: Art & Illustration

5. The protagonist in this story is _____.

   _____ Shaun

   _____ Malik

   _____ the narrator

6. What is the main idea of paragraph 1?

   _____
   _____

7. How does Shaun help Malik solve his problem?

   _____
   _____
   _____

Describe your experience saving money for something you wanted to do or buy.

_____
_____
_____
_____
_____

Spectrum Reading Grade 8

Name _____

Chapter 3: Art & Illustration

> How can people who disagree reach an understanding?

Born to Draw

Aisha scanned the calendar on her phone and sighed. Even though she looked forward to beginning eighth grade, she would miss the time spent drawing during summer vacation. In only two months, Aisha had finally developed the character concepts that, for months prior, she had only been able to see in her mind's eye. Whenever she flipped through her recent work, Aisha got chills. It was so gratifying to see how her drawings could bring life to her storytelling! The way she saw it, comic illustration was the perfect medium for her characters' story.

Unfortunately, Aisha's parents didn't understand how committed she was to becoming a comic illustrator. Her parents had no objection when Aisha's older sister decided to study law in college. Her older brother had worked for a landscape company over the summer to see if landscape architecture suited him. So, when Aisha had shared her storyboards with her parents recently, she expected them to support her. Instead, they had explained that drawing comics was a hobby, not a career.

As she was recalling that unpleasant conversation, James, her brother, knocked on the door. He said, "Aisha, Mom and Dad want you to help set the table for dinner, and I know you're not going to help me with the dishes afterward!" James's footsteps pounded down the hall.

After dinner, when Aisha began helping with the dishes, James was surprised. "Why are you being so helpful, Aisha? Washing dishes is your absolute least favorite chore, and don't pretend otherwise!"

"Hey now," Aisha began, "don't you think you should stop questioning me before I change my mind?" The siblings giggled, and Aisha continued. "Actually, I hoped you could give me some advice. You know I've been drawing comics all summer." Aisha paused before continuing. "Well, I finally decided to show Mom and Dad my work."

James looked at Aisha. "How much did they love 'The Critter Crew,' especially that crazy little squirrel and his—what did you call it—'merry murder of crow pals'? I've got to say, Aisha, that is one of the funniest stories my friends and I have ever read. I wish I had half your creativity and imagination. But I don't understand—I don't have your talent, so why are you coming to me for advice?"

54   Spectrum Reading Grade 8

Name _____

Chapter 3: Art & Illustration

"I'm not looking for advice about 'The Critter Crew,' James," Aisha responded. She was slightly annoyed; her brother sometimes really missed the point. "I want you to help me convince Mom and Dad that drawing comics is an art form, and that it can even be a great career."

But as she spoke, the look on her brother's face told her that he agreed with their parents. Aisha politely listened to her brother's response, and then she went back to her room, dejected.

At school a few weeks later, Miss Santoro noticed that Aisha wasn't herself. Aisha confessed to Miss Santoro that she was frustrated with trying to convince her parents to take her comic illustrations seriously. She explained that the way her family felt about each of their chosen paths was how she felt about illustration.

Pointing to the bookshelf in the front of the room, Miss Santoro began, "My dad got into an argument once with his sister—my aunt—who was a journalist. According to my dad, writing was not a career. When I heard that conversation, I was probably about your age. Despite my anxiety, I was straightforward with my dad. I simply told him the truth. I explained that writing was my passion, and that I wanted to get better and to write. I guess my honesty came through, and he believed me."

When Aisha heard Miss Santoro's story, it inspired her to seriously discuss her intentions with her parents. It wasn't instantaneous, but eventually, they came to understand that Aisha's love of comic illustration was more important than whether or not it was the career they wanted for Aisha.

Name _____

Chapter 3: Art & Illustration

> Answer the questions about *Born to Draw*.

1. Based on information from the story, which of the following statements is false?

   _____ Aisha is frustrated because her parents do not regard comic illustration as a realistic career choice.

   _____ Aisha is frustrated because her parents have supported her siblings' career goals, but not hers.

   _____ Aisha is frustrated because she plans to become wealthy as a comic illustrator and her parents are not supporting that goal.

   _____ Aisha is frustrated because her brother agrees with her parents.

2. Why is Aisha disappointed that the summer is coming to an end?

   _____

   _____

   _____

3. The word *storyboards* appears in paragraph 2. Write a definition for this word based on how it is used in the text.

   _____

   _____

   _____

Name _____

Chapter 3: Art & Illustration

4. Write a sentence that summarizes Miss Santoro's advice to Aisha.

   _____
   _____

5. Circle the word below that you think best describes Aisha. Then, explain on the lines that follow why you chose the word.

       creative   self-motivated   determined   angry

   _____
   _____

6. What do Miss Santoro's actions tell you about her abilities as a teacher?

   _____
   _____

> Do you think writing and illustrating comics is a realistic career choice? Why or why not?
>
> _____
> _____
> _____
> _____

Spectrum Reading Grade 8

Chapter 4: Fossils

Before Reading

Get your student ready to read with before-reading prompts and exercises.

- What do you already know about fossils?
- What is a memorable experience you've had with fossils?
- Skim through the pages of this chapter. Look at the titles of the selections, illustrations and/or photographs, italicized words, and any other text features.
- Make predictions. What do you think you will read about in this chapter?

During Reading

Encourage your student to use close-reading strategies to gain a deeper understanding of the text.

- Underline the details you find most interesting.
- How is the selection you are reading organized? Could it have been organized in a different way?
- Think about any information you think is missing from the selection.

After Reading

Your student should complete the page(s) of questions following each selection to demonstrate their comprehension of the text. Support their reading comprehension with after-reading reflection questions.

- Were your predictions correct?
- What did you learn?
- How did you connect to the text?

Helpful Definitions

Having a good grasp of the vocabulary found in a reading selection is key for reading comprehension. Before reading each definition, ask your student: *What do you think this word means? Is there another word you know that has the same root? Does the part of speech help you understand the word's meaning?*

asphalt: a black, tarlike substance that is mixed with sand and gravel and then rolled flat to make roads

excavation: the process of digging a large hole in the earth to search for something buried, as in archaeological research

specimens: samples or examples used to stand for a whole group

dioramas: scenic representations in which figures and lifelike details are displayed

expedition: a journey for a specific purpose

jack-of-all-trades: someone who can do passable work at various tasks

de-extinction: act of reversing extinction by reintroducing species

interrelated: having a reciprocal relation

preserving: the process of protecting something so that it stays in its original or current state

renovations: restorations done to something by cleaning, repairing, or remodeling

reverence: honor and respect that is felt or shown

marvel: to become filled with surprise and astonishment

faux: not real or genuine; made to look like something else that is valuable

Name _____

Chapter 4: Fossils

What kinds of historical treasures have been found in the La Brea Tar Pits?

Stuck in the Pits

Picture the busy, humming streets of Los Angeles today. Stores, skyscrapers, restaurants, taxis, convertibles, and people rushing to and fro fill the streets. The scene was very different 100,000, or even 50,000, years ago. Cracks in the ground allowed oil to seep to the surface and form pools of sticky asphalt. During warm weather, small animals and insects became trapped in it. Sometimes, they came to drink the water that collected on its surface. Other times, they simply were unlucky enough to stumble into the asphalt.

The small, trapped animals were easy prey for larger animals that happened by. Sometimes, the larger animals would become trapped too. Their weight caused their feet to sink into the asphalt. If they were young and strong, they may have had a chance at freeing themselves, but many died of exhaustion, struggling to lift their limbs from the clinging muck.

Although this was a tragic situation for the animals that died there, the La Brea Tar Pits have provided modern scientists with a wealth of information. Excavation of the tar pits began in 1913. The Hancock family, who owned the land, gave the Los Angeles County Museum the right to excavate there for two years. In just that two-year period, a million bones, from more than 300 species, were recovered. Imagine cleaning, identifying, and housing all those remains!

Since that time, paleontologists have unearthed more than three million fossils. The most common find in the pits is dire wolf bones. Dire wolves were large, prehistoric wolves that lived between 40,000 and 11,000 years ago. Scientists believe that the wolves were trapped in the asphalt when they came to feed on smaller trapped animals. Specimens of more than 4,000 dire wolves can be found at the Page Museum, which houses items found in the tar pits.

Next to dire wolves, the most common animals found are saber-toothed cats and coyotes. Like wolves, these animals were predators that were likely to have been attracted to the tar pits by the temptation of easy prey. Although the large skeletons are obviously the most dramatic finds, even the fossilized remains of plants and insects can give scientists a broader picture of what life was like long ago.

Chapter 4: Fossils

The La Brea paleontologists are often asked if they have uncovered any dinosaur fossils or if there's a chance they will. That is one question that is easy to answer—no. The oldest remains found in the tar pits are approximately 55,000 years old. Dinosaurs lived 65 million years ago, when the area surrounding the tar pits was still entirely covered by the Pacific Ocean.

One of the most interesting things about the La Brea Tar Pits is that they are still being excavated. In a world where so many mysteries have already been solved, it's exciting to know that there is still a treasure trove of uncovered specimens from this rich time in history. In 2006, the LA County Museum of Art began construction on a new parking garage. Digging for this project uncovered new fossil deposits. Among them was the nearly complete skeleton of a woolly mammoth! The new fossil deposits were placed in 23 enormous boxes, which were then moved to a site closer to the other tar pits. "Project 23," as it is known, will take paleontologists years to sort through. There is no super fast and efficient method of uncovering the remains. While the old, reliable methods of recovery still work, new chemical and excavation techniques have been developed. What more will be discovered?

Spectrum Reading Grade 8

Name _____

Chapter 4: Fossils

Answer the questions about *Stuck in the Pits*.

1. Make a check mark next to the word or words that best describe what type of nonfiction passage this is.

   _____ how-to

   _____ informational text

   _____ persuasive text

2. Is it likely that fossilized dinosaur bones will be discovered at the La Brea Tar Pits? Why or why not?

   _____

   _____

   _____

3. Paleontologists have found more _____ remains than any other animal.

   _____ dire wolf

   _____ saber-toothed cat

   _____ coyote

4. Name one cause and its effect from the selection.

   Cause: _____

   Effect: _____

62   Spectrum Reading Grade 8

Name _____

Chapter 4: Fossils

Search for this skill ID on IXL.com for more practice!

IXL.com skill ID
8HV

5. Describe what Project 23 is.

   _____
   _____
   _____
   _____

6. Excavating fossils is very different today than it was 100 years ago. Is this statement true or false? Explain.

   _____
   _____
   _____
   _____

7. How do you think the author feels about the discoveries in the La Brea Tar Pits? Cite examples from the selection to support your answer.

   _____
   _____
   _____
   _____
   _____
   _____

Spectrum Reading Grade 8

63

Name _____

Chapter 4: Fossils

What is it like to be a paleontologist?

Fossil Hunters

Although many people think of paleontologists as dinosaur hunters, searching for dinosaur fossils is only one part of the job. Paleontologists study the history of life on Earth and fossils of all kinds—from plants and cells to fish and saber-toothed cats. Dinosaurs are some of the most dramatic remains, but fossils of plants and animals from different points in time help scientists piece together a more complete picture of the history of life on our planet.

Paleontology draws heavily on geology (the study of rocks) and biology (the study of life). An in-depth knowledge of rocks is important because rocks can provide needed information about the fossils they hold. Information about layering of rocks and soil types can also be valuable. Principles of biology come into play when paleontologists date and identify the specimens they find. Imagine trying to put together the fossilized remains of an animal's skeleton. It would be like working on a puzzle without knowing what the finished picture looks like. The knowledge of other life forms gives paleontologists the background they need to form conclusions about prehistoric forms of life.

Paleontology can be exciting work. Think of finding the remains of plants and animals that have been buried for millions of years. Picture the thrilling discovery of a new creature or finding the missing piece in a mystery scientists have been trying to solve. While these are the more glamorous parts of the job, paleontology also requires a lot of painstaking work. Paleontologists can dig for long periods of time with few finds. When they do find a fossil, recovering it is often slow. To keep from damaging the fossil, great care must be used in extracting it. Working with precise tools and small brushes can help scientists remove and preserve the fossil.

Fieldwork isn't the only part of the job for paleontologists. They spend time in labs and offices, too. They analyze and study the discoveries they make. Everything must be identified and cataloged for future reference. Paleontologists also often write about their work, sharing it with other scientists and students.

Name _____

Chapter 4: Fossils

Although becoming a paleontologist takes years of school, anyone can try their hand at fossil hunting. All it takes is interest, a little knowledge, some basic tools, and of course, patience! Experts advise that quarries, roadcuts, and cliffs are good places to look for fossils. You may be able to find local paleontology groups online that can give you tips on places to look for fossils. A masonry hammer, a small chisel, a screen (for sifting out dirt), and a soft bristled brush (for cleaning the dirt off your finds) are useful tools to bring on a fossil hunt.

Experts also advise that you bring a small notebook to record information about any fossils you find. Write the location as precisely as you can. Try to also record details about the geology of the area. Include the type of rocks above and below your find. If you can make a rough sketch or take a photo, too, that can also be helpful. Chances are that any fossils you find will probably mostly be of personal interest. If you do happen to find a large fossil, however, you should contact a local museum or university. They can help retrieve it without damaging it.

Fossil hunting can be exciting and interesting work for both professionals and amateurs. There is always room to add to the body of knowledge of what Earth was like long before humans walked the planet. And the more we learn about our planet's past, the more we know about who we are and the role of living things on Earth today.

Spectrum Reading Grade 8

65

Name _____

Chapter 4: Fossils

> Answer the questions about *Fossil Hunters*.

1. Why do you think it is important to bring a notebook on a fossil hunt and record information about your find in it?

   _____
   _____
   _____

2. Name two other sciences that play a large role in paleontology.

   _____
   _____

3. In paragraph 5, the text says that quarries, cliffs, and roadcuts are good places to look for fossils. Why do you think this is?

   _____
   _____
   _____

4. Paleontologists work exclusively in the field. Is this statement true or false? Explain.

   _____
   _____
   _____

Name _____

Chapter 4: Fossils

5. Explain why the author says that paleontology can be both exciting and painstaking work.

_____
_____
_____

6. According to the selection, assembling a dinosaur skeleton can be like _____.

7. How does knowledge of biology make the process described in question 6 easier?

_____
_____
_____

After reading this selection, do you think you'll ever try fossil hunting? Explain.

_____
_____
_____
_____

Spectrum Reading Grade 8

Name _____

Chapter 4: Fossils

What will Sierra do as a new volunteer at the natural history museum?

Working with History

Sierra heaved a sigh as her mom stopped for yet another red light. Sierra was convinced that every light between her house and the Caswell Natural History Museum had been red that morning.

Sierra had waited eagerly for the last month of school to wrap up so that she could begin her summer volunteering job at the museum. A few of her friends thought it was a little odd that she was choosing to spend two mornings a week in that "dim museum that smells weird," instead of at the pool or camp or the soccer field. Maybe it was a little odd, but the museum had been one of Sierra's favorite places in the world since her grandpa first took her there when she was four. She loved the hush of the quiet rooms, the fossils and giant skeletons of prehistoric animals, and the old-fashioned-looking dioramas of deserts, tide pools, and grasslands.

Mrs. Mendoza finally pulled up in front of the museum, next to a giant bronze statue of a triceratops. Sierra eagerly started to hop out of the car, but her mom stopped her. "Could you pose for a quick picture with the dinosaur?" she asked Sierra.

Sierra patiently slung one arm around the triceratops's neck, already warm from the sun, and grinned as her mother snapped a few photos with her cell phone.

"Perfect," said Mrs. Mendoza. "I'll pick you up at 1:00 this afternoon, okay? Have a wonderful time—I can't wait to hear all about it!"

Sierra opened the heavy wooden door to the museum and stepped inside, heading down the long hallway to the offices on the left. She smiled to herself as her eyes adjusted to the dim light. Maybe it did smell a little weird.

"Hi, Mr. Rockwell," Sierra said, tapping lightly on one of the open office doors.

"Sierra, good to see you!" replied Mr. Rockwell, taking off his glasses and jumping up to shake Sierra's hand. "I was just planning a few things for you to do this morning," he said, sitting back down at his desk. "I was thinking that you'd be sort of a jack-of-all trades for the museum."

Sierra nodded. "It sounds like I'll get a chance to work in lots of different areas that way."

Name _____

Chapter 4: Fossils

"That's just what I was thinking," Mr. Rockwell agreed, "which means that we should probably get started on your tour so that you can get the lay of the land."

Sierra and Mr. Rockwell began the tour of the museum—all the exhibits that were so familiar to Sierra were different now that she saw them from the point of view of an employee. She had often listened to the recorded messages about the exhibits on headphones that were located all over the museum. Now, however, it would be part of her job to test the headphones, wipe them down with antibacterial wipes in the morning, and make sure they were returned neatly to their stands. When they visited an area that featured animals of North America, Mr. Rockwell showed Sierra a hands-on display for kids that was frequently scattered all over the floor. Sierra would need to match the plaster animal tracks back up with the stuffed animals they belonged to.

"Are you any good at following recipes?" Mr. Rockwell asked, stopping to straighten a sign. Sierra looked surprised, but she nodded. "Good," responded Mr. Rockwell, "because it would be a great help to me if you could mix up a batch of dough that our youngest day campers could use today to make fossil imprints."

Sierra grinned. "I remember doing that activity here myself not too long ago," she said. "I think I'm going to like being a jack-of-all-trades!"

Spectrum Reading Grade 8

Name _____

Chapter 4: Fossils

Answer the questions about *Working with History.*

1. What clues at the beginning of the story let you know that Sierra is feeling impatient?

   _____

   _____

   _____

2. What does Sierra like about the natural history museum?

   _____

   _____

   _____

3. Based on the text, what do you think a *jack-of-all-trades* is?

   _____

   _____

4. Do you think Sierra will enjoy her volunteering experience? Use evidence from the text to support your answer.

   _____

   _____

   _____

   _____

Name _____

Chapter 4: Fossils

5. In paragraph 10, Mr. Rockwell uses an idiom. What is it, and what does it mean?

_____
_____
_____
_____

If you were to volunteer somewhere during your summer break, what would you choose to do? Why?

_____
_____
_____
_____
_____
_____
_____

Spectrum Reading Grade 8

Chapter 4: Fossils

> Have you ever dreamed of finding buried treasure?

Sue Hendrickson

As a child, Sue Hendrickson loved to look for buried treasure. She would also stroll along sidewalks, looking at the ground and hoping to find interesting things. After high school, she worked on boats and developed a curiosity for tropical fish. She began a job as a diver off the coast of the Florida Keys.

On one of her dive expeditions, a friend of Hendrickson's showed her a piece of amber he found in a cave he explored. The piece of amber had an insect trapped inside of it, and Sue learned that it was 23 million years old. At that moment, Hendrickson knew that she wanted to search for fossils.

Hendrickson visited the same amber mine many times, finding other fossilized specimens to share with museums and universities. This connected her to paleontologists who would invite her to accompany them on digs in Peru and America.

Name _____

Chapter 4: Fossils

In 1990, she traveled to South Dakota with a team of scientists looking for dinosaur bones. One day, the team's truck got a flat tire. When the others went to get the tire fixed, Hendrickson and her dog stayed behind and went for a walk. On her walk, Hendrickson looked toward a sandstone cliff and noticed something that needed to be investigated. When the team returned, she showed them her find. In a short time, the group uncovered a bone. Over the next month, the group uncovered the biggest, most complete skeleton of a *Tyrannosaurus rex* that had ever been found.

Because of a dispute over who actually owned the fossils, the bones were packed away for years. Finally, a museum purchased the fossils from the land owner where the *T. rex* was found. The *T. rex* was named "Sue" after its discoverer. Sue is currently on display at the Field Museum in Chicago, Illinois.

Digging up Sue was not Hendrickson's only adventure. Two years later, she dove with scientists to explore a sunken ship. It was a Spanish trading ship from the 1600s. At the wreck, the scientists found hundreds of huge stone jars and more than 400 gold and silver coins. Hendrickson has also helped find ancient sunken cities and more famous ships, including some found in the Nile River sunk during the time of Queen Cleopatra.

Hendrickson has plans for more adventures. She wants to look for more dinosaur bones and hopes to find a woolly mammoth skeleton. Often, Hendrickson travels to Chicago, Illinois, her hometown. Sue Hendrickson likes to visit Sue the dinosaur whenever she can at the Field Museum.

Spectrum Reading Grade 8

Name _____

Chapter 4: Fossils

Answer the questions about *Sue Hendrickson*.

1. Which word best describes Sue Hendrickson? Cite evidence from the text to support your answer.

    stern   adventurous   quiet   funny

    _____
    _____

2. Number the following events in the order in which they happened.

    _____ Hendrickson grew up in Chicago, Illinois.

    _____ Hendrickson found a *T. rex* skeleton in South Dakota.

    _____ Hendrickson dove to explore a Spanish trading ship.

    _____ Hendrickson saw a piece of amber 23 million years old with an insect trapped inside.

    _____ Hendrickson wants to look for a woolly mammoth skeleton.

3. Why do you think Hendrickson was invited to dive with scientists to explore a sunken Spanish trading ship?

    _____
    _____
    _____
    _____

Name _____

Chapter 4: Fossils

4. How did Hendrickson find the *T. rex* bones?

_____
_____
_____
_____
_____

If you were Hendrickson, how would you have handled finding the first curious piece of the *T. rex* skeleton? Explain.

_____
_____
_____
_____
_____
_____
_____
_____

Spectrum Reading **Grade 8**

Name _____

Chapter 4: Fossils

Do scientists have the ability to recreate extinct species?

Coming Back to Life

Have you ever wondered what the world would be like if scientists were able to bring back extinct animals? Repopulating the world with dinosaurs is an interesting idea, but it's not a real possibility. In order to bring back a species that no longer exists, scientists would need a living cell or a sample of the animal's DNA. Because dinosaurs lived 65 million years ago, there are no available samples to use—the DNA is just too old. There are many other species, however, that scientists may be able to bring back.

In fact, in 2003, scientists were able to recreate the extinct Pyrenean ibex. The ibex was a sort of wild goat that lived in the Pyrenees Mountains between France and Spain. Spanish scientists had placed a radio collar on the last known ibex so that they could track her. The ibex, named Celia, died in 2000 when a tree fell on her.

Some of Celia's cells were preserved, and several years later, scientists injected them into goat cells that had been emptied of DNA. These cells were then implanted in surrogate goat mothers. Only one of the attempts they tried worked, and a baby Pyrenean ibex was born. For a brief time, scientists had managed to bring back an extinct species. Unfortunately, the baby ibex had massive health issues and died just a few minutes after birth. Although this specific instance was only a brief success, it has given scientists great hope that de-extinction is a very real possibility.

Scientists in China and Siberia are researching and working on creating a mammoth-like elephant that can live in Arctic temperatures. One reason the mammoth is a good choice for this project is that it lived in very cold habitats. The ice and snow helped to preserve parts of the animals' bodies that would have quickly decayed otherwise. Scientists drilled into frozen cliffs along a river in Russia. They were excited to find samples of mammoth bone marrow, skin, hair, and fat. A living cell could be injected into an elephant egg that had been emptied of its DNA, much the same way the goat/ibex project worked. The egg would then be inserted into a mother elephant, which is the closest living relative of the mammoth.

Chapter 4: Fossils

There are a lot of hurdles to clear before scientists will have any chance of trying to recreate the mammoth. Even the possibility of doing so, though, has created quite a debate. Some people think that humans have a responsibility to bring back extinct animals. Some species, like the Pyrenean ibex, have been hunted out of existence. For other species, their environment has been altered enough to cause them to become extinct. In addition, many things in nature are interrelated. The extinction of one species can have far-reaching effects on other species of both plants and animals.

Those who are against the idea of de-extinction believe that it is a waste of time, money, and effort. They feel that there are thousands of living species of plants and animals that are in need of protection. They believe that human resources would be better spent in locating, studying, and preserving these living animals than in trying to bring back ones that no longer exist. There are no clear answers about the rights and wrongs of de-extinction. One thing is clear, however: human beings have always loved a challenge. The idea of doing something that once seemed impossible may be too much of a temptation to resist.

Name _____

Chapter 4: Fossils

Answer the questions about *Coming Back to Life*.

1. In your own words, explain what *de-extinction* is.

   _____

   _____

2. Who was Celia?

   _____ the Pyrenean ibex that scientists created

   _____ a woolly mammoth

   _____ the last living Pyrenean ibex

3. Why can't dinosaurs be brought back from extinction?

   _____

   _____

   _____

4. Why do some people think that humans should not waste time, energy, or money on de-extinction efforts? Use the text to support your answer.

   _____

   _____

   _____

Name _____

Chapter 4: Fossils

5. On the lines below, write a summary of paragraph 4.

_____
_____
_____
_____
_____

Do you think that scientists should try to recreate extinct animals? Why or why not?

_____
_____
_____
_____
_____
_____
_____
_____

Spectrum Reading Grade 8

Chapter 4: Fossils

What will Sierra do when she must make a difficult decision at the museum?

An Ancient Memento

Sierra had been volunteering at the Caswell Natural History Museum for two weeks. She loved getting ready for work in the morning, patting the bronze triceratops on the head as she arrived, and finding out each day what her tasks would be. The week before, the Native American room had required some renovations to fix a leak in the ceiling. All the artifacts needed to be carefully packed and moved into a storage area until the repairs were made. Sierra touched the arrowheads, the birch bark canoe, the beaver skins, and the hand-thrown pottery with great reverence. This was exactly what she loved so much about the museum; it allowed her a glimpse into lives and time periods totally different from her own.

That Wednesday morning, Mr. Rockwell had asked Sierra to shelve some books in the museum's mini science library. When she had finished, her next assignment was to dust the fossils in the "hands-on science" area of the prehistoric room. Her favorite part of the room held the miniature dioramas of prehistoric life. There were different ones for various eras in time, but the one Sierra liked best held tiny cave people draped in furs in a wintry setting. A frozen lake lay at the far end of the display, and a family of early humans huddled over a tiny faux fire. Sierra paused for a few moments to marvel at the details before she moved to the hands-on area.

She carefully picked up an ammonite and dusted the ridges of stone before she returned it to the tray above its label and information card. The crinoids, or corals, were next. Finally, Sierra reached the trilobites, the bug-like creatures that always reminded her of cockroaches, even though they were more closely related to crabs and lobsters. She was returning the last one to the tray when two little boys sprinted into the room. Their father strode quickly after them, speaking in a low but stern tone. Sierra was startled by the unexpected activity, and the trilobite she was holding slipped from her hand to the polished concrete floor.

Sierra felt her face flush as she knelt to pick up the pieces. The trilobite pieces she was holding were at least 240 million years old! Why on Earth had she been entrusted with such an ancient piece of history? Sierra was certain that she would lose her position, even though she was just a volunteer. Even worse was the embarrassment she felt. She was certain that she'd never be able to return to the museum again. Sierra couldn't believe that the mood of the morning had changed so rapidly.

Name _____

Chapter 4: Fossils

Sierra briefly considered putting the pieces back on the tray, but she knew she would be unable to lie if Mr. Rockwell asked her what happened. The only thing to do was to take responsibility for what had happened. Sierra inhaled deeply and headed for Mr. Rockwell's office.

"I'm so sorry," Sierra blurted out, "but I accidentally dropped one of the trilobite fossils when I was dusting, and it broke. I can try to reimburse the museum for it if you want. I was trying really hard to be careful, but I got startled and I dropped it."

"Whoa, whoa, Sierra, please don't worry about it," said Mr. Rockwell reassuringly. "It happens all the time," he added. "We wouldn't leave anything out for patrons to touch that we couldn't stand to see break. Why don't you take the pieces of the trilobite home with you as a memento of the day you truly became a member of the museum staff. I can't think of a single person who works here who hasn't broken something at some point in time!"

Sierra breathed a sigh of relief. "I feel so much better," she admitted. She put the trilobite pieces in her bag. "I promise that this will be my one and only memento!"

Spectrum Reading Grade 8

81

Name _____

Chapter 4: Fossils

Answer the questions about *An Ancient Memento.*

1. In paragraph 1, what does *reverence* mean?

   _____

   _____

2. What is the theme of this selection?

   _____

   _____

   _____

3. In paragraph 2, *faux* means _____ .

   _____ ancient

   _____ fake

   _____ fossilized

4. Who is the protagonist in this story?

   _____

5. What is Sierra's reaction when she drops the trilobite?

   _____

   _____

82

Spectrum Reading Grade 8

Name _____

Chapter 4: Fossils

6. Circle the word that best describes Mr. Rockwell's response to Sierra. Use evidence from the text to support your answer.

       dismayed   sympathetic   regretful

_____

_____

_____

_____

Describe a time when you did something that you felt badly about. How did you handle the situation?

_____

_____

_____

_____

_____

_____

Spectrum Reading Grade 8

Chapter 5: Search and Rescue

Before Reading

Get your student ready to read with before-reading prompts and exercises.

- What do you already know about avalanches?
- What do you already know about search and rescue teams?
- Skim through the pages of this chapter. Look at the titles of the selections, illustrations and/or photographs, italicized words, and any other text features.
- Make predictions. What do you think you will read about in this chapter?

During Reading

Encourage your student to use close-reading strategies to gain a deeper understanding of the text.

- Visualize what is happening in the reading selection while you are reading it. If it is fiction, create the characters and setting in your mind and watch the story play out as you read it.
- Annotate the text with question marks for anything confusing, underlines for anything important, and exclamation marks for anything surprising.
- After you read each paragraph, write a check mark next to it if you understood everything. Write a question mark if there was anything you did not understand. Reread any paragraphs you write a question mark next to.

After Reading

Your student should complete the page(s) of questions following each selection to demonstrate their comprehension of the text. Support their reading comprehension with after-reading reflection questions.

- Were your predictions correct?
- What did you learn?
- How did you connect to the text?

Helpful Definitions

Having a good grasp of the vocabulary found in a reading selection is key for reading comprehension. Before reading each definition, ask your student: *What do you think this word means? Is there another word you know that has the same root? Does the part of speech help you understand the word's meaning?*

terrain: a piece of land, ground

buffer: something that serves as a protective barrier

sluff: a cast off

dense: crowded

provisions: a stock of needed supplies

acquaintance: a person whom one knows but who is not a particularly close friend

unscathed: not injured

circumstances: situations

snowpack: accumulation of snow

transmitter: a device that sends out radio or television signals

Name _____

Chapter 5: Search and Rescue

How do avalanches occur?

Hidden Danger

As snow accumulates on a car windshield, it sticks to the cold surface of the window. When the driver turns the ignition and starts the car, the windshield begins to warm from the increased temperature in the car's interior. As the temperature rises, the snow on the windshield begins to slide off, sometimes in large chunks. Although the driver might not recognize it, an avalanche has just occurred on the windshield!

A windshield avalanche imitates what is known as a slab, or large scale, avalanche. However, it is not the deadly force of nature that occurs during an avalanche in a large area. A real avalanche is one of the most powerful natural events. Its formation depends upon three factors: snow, a sloped surface, and a trigger. A snowy slope with an angle between 30° and 45° is considered a potential avalanche site. The first day following a heavy, sudden snowfall over 12 inches is prime time for an avalanche to form.

Several natural circumstances can cause an avalanche. An environment with forests is much safer than open terrain. The trees create a natural buffer to anchor snow and prevent it from causing an avalanche. Valleys or sloped areas are possible danger zones, as they can quickly accumulate large amounts of snow.

The condition of snow layers in a snowpack, or accumulation of snow, also influences the likelihood of an avalanche. In areas that are quite snowy, snowpack consists of several layers of snow that have developed over time. The types of bonds throughout the snowpack's layers can determine whether an avalanche might occur. If the snow crystals do not create a strong bond, they create a weak layer in the snowpack. If the weak layer exists near the surface, it may cause a sluff, or small slide of dry, powdery snow. If the weakened layer is at the base of a snowpack, it can result in a deadly slab avalanche. Dramatic changes in temperature also can cause melting in the snowpack, causing weak bonds.

Many natural events can trigger an avalanche. However, it is estimated that about 90% of avalanches are caused by human activity. Skiers, snowboarders, and snowmobilers all depend upon snowpack to enjoy their sport. If they are not careful, their activities can result in an avalanche.

Chapter 5: Search and Rescue

Areas with smooth, steep slopes and few obstacles create an ideal setting for an avalanche. Winter sports enthusiasts seek out these exact conditions. They must use extreme caution in order to ensure their safety. Usually, these types of areas will provide signs to warn people of dangerous conditions. Most parks also offer websites or hotlines with avalanche forecasts.

Of course, skiers or snowboarders who are in avalanche-prone areas should be aware of their surroundings at all times. A partner should always be present. If travel in an area that is potentially dangerous is required, it should occur above the avalanche zone, not through the center. Basic equipment, such as shovels, rescue beacons, and avalanche probes, is essential and should be present during any such activity.

In areas where many people gather to enjoy snow sports, such as ski resorts, there are methods to control the likelihood of avalanches. One example is avalanche control teams, whose job it is to trigger controlled avalanches. They do this with explosives or by using a cannon. These methods clear the area of new snow, which can overwhelm a sturdy snowpack. This, in turn, prevents an avalanche from occurring when people are using the area for recreation. An avalanche can be a powerful and deadly force, but with caution and a little luck, most winter athletes will never encounter one.

Spectrum Reading Grade 8

Name _____

Chapter 5: Search and Rescue

Answer the questions about *Hidden Danger*.

1. In the selection, the author uses an analogy to compare two things. What are they?

   _____
   _____

2. How does the analogy add to your understanding of avalanches?

   _____
   _____
   _____

3. The three elements necessary for avalanche formation are:

   _____   _____   _____

4. What is *snowpack*?

   _____
   _____

5. Where is an avalanche more likely to occur—in a wooded area or on open terrain? Why?

   _____
   _____
   _____

Name _____

Chapter 5: Search and Rescue

6. Is the author presenting a particular point of view in this selection, or do they just present the facts?

   _____

   _____

7. What can create a weak layer in snowpack?

   _____

   _____

Do you think that skiing or snowboarding in avalanche-prone areas is too risky? Explain.

_____

_____

_____

_____

_____

_____

Spectrum Reading Grade 8

Name _____

Chapter 5: Search and Rescue

> What does Benjamin do as part of the avalanche ski patrol?

An Avalanche for Breakfast

Santiago carried napkins and silverware to the table while his mother, Mrs. Hernandez, stirred the scrambled eggs and flipped the frying pieces of bacon. Santiago's older brother, Benjamin, entered the kitchen, rubbing his eyes and stretching his arms above his head.

"That smells fantastic, Mom," Benjamin said. "I haven't had a home-cooked meal in forever. I end up eating most of my meals at a little diner a couple of blocks from my apartment."

"Absolutely my pleasure," Mrs. Hernandez replied. "Santiago and I are glad you got to come home for a few days, considering it's still ski season. I figured we wouldn't have you back here until sometime in May."

"I wasn't the only new employee hired for the patrol this season, so we have more flexibility compared to the patrollers last year."

The three filled their plates and sat at the table to eat breakfast. Santiago couldn't wait to hear about his brother's new job.

"Have you seen any avalanches yet?" Santiago asked.

"Lots, because our job is to make avalanches occur. We ski around the mountain looking for potential problem spots, and when we find one, we make sure the mountainside is evacuated, and then we use explosives to shake the snow and make it fall downhill."

"That sounds pretty dangerous," Mrs. Hernandez said worriedly.

"It is, but we all work together to make it as safe as possible. We work in teams and watch out for each other, and everyone wears a transmitter device that sends out radio signals. If someone does end up buried in the snow, we can locate them and dig them out by following the radio signals."

Santiago was trying to figure out what causes avalanches. "So, when the snow piles up too high, does it get too heavy and fall downhill? Is that an avalanche?"

Chapter 5: Search and Rescue

"Not exactly," Benjamin explained, "it has to do more with the layers of snow. Each time it snows, a new layer is created, and the layers can have different consistencies. One layer might be wetter and slushier, while another layer is frozen solid, and another is light and fluffy.

"If something disturbs the top layer, like a person walking or skiing on it, then the top layer can suddenly let loose and start sliding downhill across the layer below it. That's an avalanche. When that top layer of snow breaks free and starts racing downhill, gravity can quickly get it moving up to about 80 miles per hour. All that heavy snow tumbling downhill can cause a lot of damage, and anything in its path gets buried. You can see why the avalanche ski patrol is an important job."

"No kidding," Santiago agreed. "So, what happens when someone who isn't wearing a radio transmitter gets buried?"

"Then, we bring out our secret weapons: the dogs and drones," Benjamin continued. "We have German shepherds that we send out onto the mountainside. They have an amazing sense of smell, and they use it to find where people might be buried. Then, they race back to us and guide the patrol to where they think someone might be located under the snow. We use long poles to carefully poke down into the snow until we hit something solid, and then we start digging. I've done quite a few training exercises with the dogs, where volunteers are buried safely in the snow, and then we use the dogs to find them. Or we can use heat-seeking drones. These detect heat given off by people buried in the snow. These are especially good to use on terrain that is too dangerous for human search and rescue teams to traverse."

Santiago went to the stove and came back with the pan of scrambled eggs. He tipped it over his plate, and as the eggs tumbled from the pan onto his plate, he yelled, "Egg-valanche!"

Benjamin and Mrs. Hernandez rolled their eyes at each other, and then they started to laugh.

Name _____

Chapter 5: Search and Rescue

Answer the questions about *An Avalanche for Breakfast*.

1. Why is Benjamin home visiting his mother and brother? Place a check mark beside the best answer.

   _____ It is Santiago's birthday.   _____ Benjamin lost his job with the ski patrol.

   _____ Ski season is over.   _____ The story does not explain.

2. Identify the author's two main purposes for writing the story.

   _____
   _____
   _____
   _____

3. How does the ski patrol reduce the risk of avalanches?

   _____
   _____
   _____
   _____

4. Complete the sentence.

   The story is told from _____ point of view.

Name _____

Chapter 5: Search and Rescue

5. As indicated, provide either a cause or an effect to complete each cause-and-effect relationship from the story.

   Cause: _____

   Effect: *A long pole is carefully poked down into the snow.*

   Cause: *Eggs tumbled from the pan onto Santiago's plate.*

   Effect: _____

   Cause: _____

   Effect: *Benjamin explained what causes an avalanche.*

6. Why do the ski patrol members wear radio-transmitting devices?

   _____
   _____

7. Describe the role dogs play during an avalanche rescue operation.

   _____
   _____
   _____
   _____

Spectrum Reading Grade 8

93

Name _____

Chapter 5: Search and Rescue

Will two ski patrol rescue dogs find skiers buried by an avalanche?

Canine Rescue

The Henry family—Richard, Leah, Mitchell, and Elizabeth—had been saving all year for their vacation at a ski resort in the Rocky Mountains. On their first afternoon, they planned which slopes they wanted to ski that day and then quickly changed into their ski clothes. As the family made its way through the crowded lobby, Elizabeth noticed two ski patrollers. Each patroller was walking with a dog wearing a jacket that read "Dog Rescue." Elizabeth and Mitchell, who were already missing their own dogs, ran over.

"Hi, my name is Elizabeth, and this is my brother, Mitchell," Elizabeth said to the female patroller. "Are these really rescue dogs?"

"They remind me of our dogs, Mac and Spike, back home," commented Mitchell.

"I'm Katherine, and yes, both Aspen and Shadow are certified Avalanche Rescue Dogs with our ski patrol team. They are incredibly important to our Search and Rescue Department."

"How did Aspen and Shadow become rescue dogs?" asked Elizabeth.

"Well, certain breeds of dogs are more suited for this type of work and a lot of training is involved, too," began Enrique, the other patroller. "Aspen and Shadow's stories are special. They are rescue dogs who were rescued from a local animal shelter."

Katherine continued, "Dogs have been involved in avalanche rescue for almost 80 years. Since then, training programs and techniques have improved. Dogs can detect human scent much more quickly than humans can. And they can search much more quickly too. It's been documented that one rescue dog is equivalent to about 20 human searchers on foot."

"Many avalanche survivors have been saved by avalanche rescue dogs like Aspen and Shadow here," added Enrique proudly. "Aspen and Shadow have been working since . . . ." Enrique was caught off guard by the sound of his walkie-talkie calling out a report. Both Aspen and Shadow came to full attention.

Richard's and Leah's faces looked both excited and concerned as they heard the words coming through. "Avalanche reported in Area 12. Two backcountry skiers reported missing." With no further words, Enrique, Katherine, Aspen, and Shadow disappeared into the crowd.

94

Spectrum Reading Grade 8

Chapter 5: Search and Rescue

Apparently, slightly rising temperatures over the last week had caused instability near one of the outer ski areas. The snowpack had weakened, and the mere presence and weight of skiers could easily trigger an avalanche. Fortunately for the ski patrol, this exercise was just a drill. It is important to always be prepared when conditions present possible dangers.

The rescue patrol arrived on the scene, and Aspen and Shadow got to work sniffing out the area, trying to locate scent pools. Within minutes, Aspen began digging rapidly.

"He's on it!" hollered Enrique. "Good boy, Aspen!"

The ski patrol team went to work in Aspen's area, and within 30 minutes they had located and freed one of the buried skiers. The other skier was located nearby 10 minutes later. Word quickly spread back to the lodge that the drill was a success and both skiers were located by the dogs. The news also spread that Aspen had almost immediately pinpointed the exact spot of the first skier rescued.

"I can't wait to tell all my friends!" said Elizabeth.

"I hope we get to see Aspen and Shadow again to give them some extra special pets and hugs," added Mitchell.

"I agree," said Richard. "After talking with Katherine and Enrique today, and learning about avalanche rescue dogs, it doesn't surprise me at all that Aspen is a hero!"

Name _____

Chapter 5: Search and Rescue

Answer the questions about *Canine Rescue*.

1. In paragraph 7, *documented* means

   _____ explained.

   _____ recorded; proven.

   _____ disputed.

2. What signal did the sound of the walkie-talkies send to Aspen and Shadow?

   _____
   _____

3. On the lines below, write one fact and one opinion from the story.

   Fact: _____

   Opinion: _____

4. What advantage do search and rescue dogs have over humans?

   _____
   _____

5. In paragraph 11, what do you think *scent pools* means?

   _____
   _____

Name _____

Chapter 5: Search and Rescue

6. Make a check mark next to the words you would most likely use when describing a ski patroller.

   ____ courageous   ____ suspicious   ____ fussy   ____ dependable

   ____ conceited   ____ athletic   ____ energetic   ____ studious

7. Cite examples from the story that indicate how Elizabeth and Mitchell feel about dogs.

   _____
   _____
   _____
   _____

8. What is the climax of the story?

   _____
   _____
   _____

9. What is the story's resolution?

   _____
   _____
   _____

Spectrum Reading Grade 8

Chapter 6: Let's Eat

Before Reading

Get your student ready to read with before-reading prompts and exercises.

- What do you already know about being a chef?
- What do you know about different cuisines?
- Skim through the pages of this chapter. Look at the titles of the selections, illustrations and/or photographs, italicized words, and any other text features.
- Make predictions. What do you think you will read about in this chapter?

During Reading

Encourage your student to use close-reading strategies to gain a deeper understanding of the text.

- Think about what would have been another good illustration or photo for the selection as you read.
- How did the author begin the selection? Why do you think they chose to start it like that?
- After reading a few paragraphs of a selection, has your prediction for what it is about changed?

After Reading

Your student should complete the page(s) of questions following each selection to demonstrate their comprehension of the text. Support their reading comprehension with after-reading reflection questions.

- Were your predictions correct?
- What did you learn?
- How did you connect to the text?

Helpful Definitions

Having a good grasp of the vocabulary found in a reading selection is key for reading comprehension. Before reading each definition, ask your student: *What do you think this word means? Is there another word you know that has the same root? Does the part of speech help you understand the word's meaning?*

aspired: sought after to get; accomplished a goal

enlist: to secure support of; enroll

deemed: thought of, judged, considered

culinary: of or relating to the kitchen

revelation: a pleasant surprise

candidate: one likely chosen or qualified for a certain role

acclaimed: praised

experimental: of or relating to an experiment

authentic: real; actual

condiment: something added to food such as a seasoning, sauce, or topping to add to its flavor

wasabi: a condiment prepared from the rhizome of a Japanese herb; similar to horseradish

garnish: savory touch to food or drink

versatile: having many uses or applications

Chapter 6: Let's Eat

> How did an American-born woman become *The French Chef?*

Julia Child

Julia McWilliams, who would later in life be known around the world as the French Chef, Julia Child, was born in Pasadena, California, in 1912. She was an active, athletic young woman who played tennis, golf, and basketball, but cooking was not yet on her mind. She mostly aspired to be a writer, and so, when she graduated from Smith College in 1934, it was with a degree in English. Child headed to New York City and began a career in advertising as a copywriter.

The attack on Pearl Harbor in 1941 brought the United States into World War II. Like many other Americans, Child wanted to serve her country. She attempted to enlist in either the Army or the Navy, but her height of six feet two inches was deemed too tall for either service. Instead, Child found a job with the Office of Strategic Services, or the OSS, known today as the CIA. She began as a typist, but she quickly rose in the ranks due to her intelligence and drive. Soon Child was working as a top researcher, answering to General Donovan, head of the OSS.

Name _____

Chapter 6: Let's Eat

Child's assignments took her to China and other Asian nations. While stationed in Ceylon, now called Sri Lanka, she met another OSS employee, the man who would become her lifelong best friend and husband: Paul Child. The two were married in 1946. Two years later, they moved to Paris, France, and Julia Child's culinary life began.

After eating at France's oldest restaurant, La Couronne, Child had a revelation. She described the experience as "an opening up of the soul and spirit for me." She knew food and cooking were her passions, and she pursued her passion by enrolling in the world-famous Le Cordon Bleu cooking school. She also worked privately with master chefs and joined a women's cooking club.

Through the cooking club, Child met two French women who were working to compile a master volume of French recipes. They hoped that Child would be able to work with them to make the book appealing to Americans. With her experiences as a cook, an English major, and an American citizen, she seemed to be the perfect candidate.

The women worked together on the book for 10 years. Several times it was rejected for being too big or too much like an encyclopedia. But finally, in 1961, the massive, 726-page *Mastering the Art of French Cooking* was published in the United States. It seemed an unlikely candidate for popular success. However, the cookbook was critically acclaimed and topped the bestseller lists. French cooking swept the nation.

By then, Julia and Paul lived in Cambridge, Massachusetts. Based on the popularity of her book, Child was invited to cook live on the air as a guest on a public television show in Boston. Her segment was so popular, the station decided to invite her back to host her own cooking show. Today, entire TV networks are dedicated to airing cooking and food-related programming. But in 1963, this idea was brand new. *The French Chef* debuted to immediate success, and the era of cooking shows was born.

Child's show ran for the next 10 years. She continued writing, making public appearances, and, of course, cooking for the rest of her life. When Julia Child died in 2004, a couple of days shy of her 92nd birthday, she was arguably the most famous chef—French or otherwise—in the entire world.

Name _____

Chapter 6: Let's Eat

Answer the questions about *Julia Child*.

1. Which genre of nonfiction best describes the text? Place a check mark on the line of the correct answer.

   _____ autobiography   _____ biography

   _____ historical nonfiction   _____ essay

2. How did the author organize the information in the text? Do you think this was a good choice? Why or why not?

   _____
   _____
   _____
   _____

3. Reread the focus question above the title. Write a few sentences that answer the question based on information from the text.

   _____
   _____
   _____
   _____
   _____
   _____

Name _____

Chapter 6: Let's Eat

4. Why did Julia Child and her cowriters have trouble publishing *Mastering the Art of French Cooking*?

   _____

   _____

5. Which of the following statements is true? Place a check mark on the line of the true statement.

   _____ From the time she was young, Julia Child always dreamed of being a famous chef.

   _____ Julia Child worked as a spy for the CIA during World War II.

   _____ *Mastering the Art of French Cooking* was the book that inspired Julia Child to become a chef.

   _____ Julia Child's first television show was called *The French Chef*.

   What are you passionate about? How do you pursue your passions?

   _____

   _____

   _____

   _____

Spectrum Reading Grade 8

Name _____

Chapter 6: Let's Eat

What steps will lead you to a delicious baguette?

Julia's Famous French Bread

Equipment needed:
electric mixer with bowl, baking sheet, linen towel, baking stone, oven

Ingredients:

1 packet of instant yeast

$3\frac{1}{2}$ cups all-purpose flour

$2\frac{1}{4}$ teaspoons salt

$1\frac{1}{2}$ cups warm water (approximately 125°F)

Preparation time: approximately 10 hours

Directions:

1. In a mixing bowl, combine the yeast, $2\frac{1}{2}$ cups of flour, and the salt. Using a flat beater in the electric mixer, mix the ingredients on low for about half a minute.

2. Continue mixing on low as you pour in the water.

3. After the dough has just begun to thicken, clean off the flat beater, and replace it with a dough hook. Mix in the remaining 1 cup of flour, adding a little at a time until you have a soft, smooth dough that is a bit sticky. It should take about 5 minutes, and you may not need all the flour.

4. Remove the dough from the bowl and set it aside while you clean and dry the bowl.

5. Place the dough back in the bowl, and allow it to rise at room temperature for about 3 hours. When it has finished rising, the dough should be about 3–4 times its original size.

6. Using your fist, push down the dough into the bowl several times to deflate it. Then, reform the dough into a ball and place it back into the bowl. Let the dough rise again at room temperature for a couple of hours. When the dough is ready, it will be about $2\frac{1}{2}$–3 times the original size.

Name _____

Chapter 6: Let's Eat

7. While the dough is rising, place a linen towel onto a baking sheet, and rub flour into the towel's fabric.

8. Once the dough has finished rising for the second time, divide it into several equal pieces, depending on how large you want your finished loaves to be. Shape each loaf, and place all of them on the towel-covered baking sheet. Loosely cover the loaves and let them rise for a third time, for approximately 2 hours.

9. Preheat your oven to 450°F. Place a baking stone on the center rack and allow it to heat with the oven.

10. Once the loaves have finished rising for the last time, slash each loaf diagonally across the top 2 or 3 times with a small knife. Spray the loaves with water. Then, place the loaves onto the preheated baking stone.

11. Bake the loaves for about 25 minutes, or until they are golden brown. While they are baking, spray the loaves lightly with water 3 times at approximately 5-minute intervals.

12. Allow the loaves to cool for a couple of hours before you try to cut them.

13. Enjoy your delicious baguettes!

Name _____

Chapter 6: Let's Eat

> Answer the questions about *Julia's Famous French Bread*.

1. Identify the author's main purpose for writing the text. Place a check mark on the line of the correct answer.

   _____ to entertain the reader   _____ to inform the reader

   _____ to convince the reader   _____ to explain to the reader

2. How does the text's organizational structure support the author's purpose?

   _____

   _____

   _____

3. Why do you think the ingredients list is placed near the beginning of the text rather than near the end?

   _____

   _____

4. Approximately how much time does the dough need to rise in total? Place a check mark on the line of the correct answer.

   _____ 3 hours   _____ 7 hours

   _____ 5 hours   _____ 10 hours

106   Spectrum Reading Grade 8

Name _____

Chapter 6: Let's Eat

5. Which step occurs immediately after the third and final rising of the dough? Place a check mark on the line of the correct answer.

   _____ Shape the dough into loaves.　　　_____ Place the loaves into the oven.

   _____ Slash the loaves diagonally.　　　_____ Spray the loaves with water.

6. Based on the steps and time involved, how would you describe this recipe in terms of difficulty?

   _____

   _____

Describe a time when you followed steps to complete a process. Were the steps clearly described? Was the end result a success?

_____

_____

_____

_____

_____

_____

_____

Spectrum Reading Grade 8

Name _____

Chapter 6: Let's Eat

What egg recipes do you like to prepare?

Garden Veggie Frittata

Ingredients:
1 tablespoon olive oil
1 large Yukon Gold potato, peeled and thinly sliced
2 green onions, sliced
1 red pepper, seeded and chopped
1 cup baby spinach, chopped
1 teaspoon minced garlic
8 eggs
1 tablespoon chopped fresh basil, plus more for garnish
1 cup shredded cheddar cheese
salt and pepper to taste

* Safety Reminder:
Remember to wash all vegetables before you begin cooking, and wash your hands after you handle raw eggs.

Additional Materials:
oven-safe pan or skillet, sharp knife, whisk, measuring cup, cutting board

Directions:
1. Preheat the oven to 375°F.

2. Heat half a tablespoon of olive oil in a large skillet over medium heat. Add the sliced potatoes to the pan, and sauté them until they are tender but firm (about 6 minutes). Remove the potatoes from the pan. Put the rest of the olive oil in the pan, and then add the green onions, red pepper, spinach, and garlic. Sauté just until the spinach is wilted. Season the vegetables with salt and pepper.

3. In a medium bowl, beat together the eggs, basil, and cheddar cheese with a whisk. Pour into the pan over the vegetables. Reduce heat to medium low, and scramble the eggs for about a minute. Return the potatoes to the pan, and cook for an additional 2 to 3 minutes. You should notice the eggs starting to set around the edges.

Chapter 6: Let's Eat

4. Place the pan in the preheated oven, and bake for 10 to 12 minutes, until the eggs have completely set in the center. Loosen the frittata with a spatula, and then flip it onto a serving plate. Garnish it with some of the fresh basil. Slice and serve while warm. Serves four.

Serving Suggestion:
This frittata is a tasty, versatile dish that can be served at any time of day. Serve it for breakfast or lunch with a slice of toast and a fruit salad. At dinner, add a baguette and side salad, and you'll be all set.

Name _____

Chapter 6: Let's Eat

> Answer the questions about *Garden Veggie Frittata.*

1. For what purpose is the asterisk (*) used in the text?

   _____

   _____

2. Which ingredients could be omitted, based on preference?

   _____

   _____

3. In step 2, what does the word *sauté* mean?

   _____

   _____

4. In step 4, what does the word *garnish* mean?

   _____

   _____

5. In step 3, the author says that *you should notice the eggs starting to set around the edges.* What does this mean?

   _____

   _____

Name _____

Chapter 6: Let's Eat

6. Number the following steps in the order in which they should be completed in the recipe.

   _____ Remove the potatoes from the pan.

   _____ Sauté the potatoes in olive oil.

   _____ Preheat the oven.

   _____ Loosen the frittata with a spatula.

   _____ Scramble the eggs for a minute.

   _____ Season the vegetables with salt and pepper.

   Is this a recipe you would like to try? Why or why not?

   _____
   _____
   _____
   _____
   _____
   _____
   _____
   _____

Name _____

Chapter 6: Let's Eat

> How will Alex and Emily feel about trying a new cuisine?

An Experimental Appetite

A new Japanese restaurant had just opened up in town and Alex and Emily Godfrey were trying it out. Alex loved to try new foods. He liked Chinese food, but had never been to a Japanese restaurant before. He wondered if it would be similar since they were both Asian cuisines.

Emily wasn't as confident as Alex was about trying new foods. Alex would eat practically anything and not think twice about it. Emily liked to be able to identify everything on her plate. She was willing to try new things, but she lacked Alex's enthusiasm for experimenting with new foods.

"Have you looked at the menu yet?" asked Alex and Emily's dad.

"I don't see anything I like," said Emily.

Mr. Godfrey grinned. "That shouldn't stop you from looking at it," he said. "Maybe our waiter, Mr. Ito, can give us some suggestions."

"Of course I can," he said. "How about you start off with some sushi? Do you like fish?" he asked Alex and Emily.

"I do," replied Alex promptly.

Emily looked uncertainly at her parents. "I like some kinds of fish," she said.

"She likes fish that doesn't have a strong fishy taste to it," added her mom helpfully.

"I'll bring you several different kinds," said Mr. Ito. "Then, you'll have a chance to sample them and decide what you like. Do you know how sushi is made?" Mr. Ito asked Alex and Emily. They shook their heads. "Well, the sushi chef begins with a very thin sheet of seaweed."

"We're going to eat seaweed?" asked Alex excitedly.

Mr. Ito smiled. "You wouldn't even know it was seaweed if I didn't tell you," he said.

Name _____

Chapter 6: Let's Eat

Mr. Ito continued, "The chef spreads a layer of sticky rice over the seaweed. Then, they add different vegetables and fish. They roll everything up inside the seaweed and slice it into little disks."

A few minutes later, Mr. Ito returned with a wooden board that held several different types of sushi.

"You might want to try this kind first," Mr. Ito told Emily. "It has cucumber and avocado in it but no fish." Mr. Ito showed the Godfreys how to pick up the sushi using chopsticks.

"What's this?" asked Alex, pointing to a small mound of something green.

"Sushi is often served with pickled ginger and a very spicy condiment called wasabi," Mrs. Godfrey said. The green stuff you were asking about is the wasabi. If you decide to try some, you'll probably want to use a very small amount at first."

No one at the table was surprised to learn that Alex loved the sushi. He even found that he liked wasabi, as long as he was careful to use only a small speck of it on each bite.

"What do you think, Emily?" asked Mrs. Godfrey after a few moments.

Emily picked up another piece of sushi with her chopsticks. "I love it," she said. "I think we're going to need to find more restaurants where I can try new cuisines," she added.

Mr. and Mrs. Godfrey laughed. "Our kids are turning into very well-seasoned eaters!" said Mr. Godfrey.

Spectrum Reading Grade 8

Name _____

Chapter 6: Let's Eat

Answer the questions about *An Experimental Appetite*.

1. Write **F** before the sentences that are facts. Write **O** before the sentences that are opinions.

   _____ Sushi is delicious.

   _____ The chef spreads a layer of sticky rice over the sheet of seaweed.

   _____ Wasabi ruins the flavor of sushi.

   _____ Mr. Ito makes some suggestions about what to order.

2. How are Alex and Emily different?

   _____
   _____
   _____

3. Why isn't everyone surprised that Alex likes sushi?

   _____
   _____
   _____

4. What holds everything together in a roll of sushi?

   _____
   _____

Name _____

Chapter 6: Let's Eat

5. How would changing the word *excitedly* to *hesitantly* in the following sentence affect the text?

   "We're going to eat seaweed?" asked Alex excitedly.

   _____

   _____

6. Why does Mr. Godfrey say, "Our kids are turning into some well-seasoned eaters"? Use evidence from the text to explain your answer.

   _____

   _____

   _____

> How would you describe your favorite food to someone who has never tried it?
>
> _____
>
> _____
>
> _____
>
> _____
>
> _____
>
> _____
>
> _____

Spectrum Reading Grade 8

Chapter 7: Space

Before Reading

Get your student ready to read with before-reading prompts and exercises.

- What do you already know about space?
- What do you want to learn about space?
- Skim through the pages of this chapter. Look at the titles of the selections, illustrations and/or photographs, italicized words, and any other text features.
- Make predictions. What do you think you will read about in this chapter?

During Reading

Encourage your student to use close-reading strategies to gain a deeper understanding of the text.

- Think about what would have been another good illustration or photo for the selection as you read.
- How did the author begin the selection? Why do you think they chose to start it like that?
- After reading a few paragraphs of a selection, has your prediction for what it is about changed?

After Reading

Your student should complete the page(s) of questions following each selection to demonstrate their comprehension of the text. Support their reading comprehension with after-reading reflection questions.

- Were your predictions correct?
- What did you learn?
- How did you connect to the text?

Helpful Definitions

Having a good grasp of the vocabulary found in a reading selection is key for reading comprehension. Before reading each definition, ask your student: *What do you think this word means? Is there another word you know that has the same root? Does the part of speech help you understand the word's meaning?*

atrial: of, or relating to, the chamber in the heart that receives blood from the veins

fibrillation: very rapid irregular contractions of the muscle fibers of the heart

cardiac: of, or relating to, the heart

rover: a vehicle for exploring the surface of an extraterrestrial body, such as the moon or Mars

sediment: the matter that settles to the bottom of liquid

microbial: filled with microorganisms or germs

immensity: the state of being very large

simulated: made to look real

psychological: of, relating to, or occurring in the mind

desolate: deserted with no living beings

grim: somber, gloomy

Spectrum Reading Grade 8

Name _____

Chapter 7: Space

How can an experiment conducted in space help humans stay healthy?

Planting a Seed for the Future

Jessica stopped in her tracks as she saw the NASA poster in the hallway at school. Her friend Juan barely avoided bumping into her and looked to see what was capturing her attention.

"Did you see this?" asked Jessica. "What an awesome opportunity!" She looked at the details of the contest that the poster was publicizing. One lucky student would have his or her experiment performed in space. The deadline for the contest was in just a few weeks, though. Jessica sighed, thinking it would be impossible for her to even brainstorm an idea for a project in a few weeks, much less design an entire experiment.

Jessica had biology class next period, and she stayed a few minutes to talk to her teacher, Mrs. Butcher. "Do you have any idea what I could do for an experiment for the NASA contest?"

Mrs. Butcher looked at Jessica thoughtfully. "Well, Jessica, I can't tell you specifically what to do, but maybe you could consider an experiment that will benefit people's health. Many plants are used in medical treatments. You could think about doing an experiment using one of them."

Jessica grinned. "Thanks Mrs. B., you've given me the seed of a thought!" As she walked away, she heard Mrs. Butcher chuckling. Jessica headed to the library and asked the librarian to help her find books about plant science, or botany. The librarian found one that contained a chapter on plants used in medications, and Jessica's eye was immediately drawn to the picture of foxglove that she saw on the second page. She thought with excitement, *I'm almost positive that Mom has that in our garden! I wonder what it's used for.*

After reading further, Jessica discovered that foxglove, scientifically called *digitalis*, is used in the treatment of irregular heartbeats because it strengthens heart contractions. Despite being a toxic plant, foxglove was obviously valuable to heart patients and Jessica thought that finding more efficient ways to grow the plant might reduce the price of the medication produced from it. She decided that her experiment would focus on finding out if foxglove would grow more rapidly in a reduced gravity environment.

Chapter 7: Space

Jessica ran her idea by Mrs. Butcher, who approved it and asked her to come up with the method that she would use to design and perform her experiment. As Jessica bounced back to the library, she grabbed a dictionary off the shelf. Words like *atrial, fibrillation,* and *cardiac* were coming up regularly in her research, which was a little intimidating, and she wanted to be able to use them correctly as she developed her experiment. Juan found her there, and Jessica excitedly explained that she thought foxglove plants would grow faster in reduced gravity. In the next few weeks, she planned to design an experiment that evaluated how different light, soil, and moisture levels can affect the growth of foxglove plants.

A week before the deadline, Jessica brought her project outline and completed contest entry form to Mrs. Butcher. Mrs. Butcher was eager to comment on her work, and Jessica made the few changes her teacher suggested. Jessica carefully packed up her completed experiment details and shipped them via registered mail to NASA. It would be several months before the winner of the contest was announced, but with the hard work behind her, she wasn't bothered a bit.

Jessica found Juan shooting baskets on his driveway. "I think we need to go celebrate," she said, grabbing the ball and dribbling a few times before she attempted a shot. "My work is done. The next step is . . . space!" she said, sinking a basket.

Juan grinned and bumped fists with her. "That definitely calls for ice cream," he cheered.

Spectrum Reading Grade 8

Name _____

Chapter 7: Space

> Answer the questions about *Planting a Seed for the Future*.

1. What is the hypothesis in Jessica's experiment?

   _____
   _____

2. How does Jessica's attitude about the contest change between the beginning and end of the story?

   _____
   _____
   _____

3. Why does Jessica decide to use foxglove in her experiment?

   _____
   _____

4. Why does Mrs. Butcher laugh when Jessica says, "You've given me the seed of a thought"?

   _____
   _____

5. Why is Jessica's experiment well suited to being performed in space?

   _____
   _____

Name _____

Chapter 7: Space

6. Find and write parts of the story that can be categorized by these distinctions.

Propel Action	Reveal Character	Provoke Decisions

Name _____

Chapter 7: Space

> What can scientists learn about Mars using only a robot?

Curiosity in Space

On a partly cloudy day in November 2011, a 15-story-tall rocket lifted off from the Cape Canaveral Air Force Station in Florida. The spacecraft perched atop the rocket was destined for Mars. It contained one the most complex pieces of machinery ever developed by NASA (National Aeronautics and Space Administration). After the rockets fell away, the spacecraft—called the Mars Science Laboratory—traveled through space for the next eight months with its precious cargo: a car-sized robotic rover called *Curiosity*.

On August 6, 2012, *Curiosity* landed safely at the Bradbury Landing Site, named after science fiction writer Ray Bradbury. The rover would be sending information back to Earth about the Martian landscape and climate. Specifically, scientists hoped to find signs that life may have once existed on the planet. Water plays a vital role in allowing life to exist, so one of the first steps was to investigate evidence of water on Mars. The landing site was carefully chosen so *Curiosity* could fulfill this mission.

The Bradbury Landing Site is located in the Gale Crater. By studying the geography of Mars, scientists believed the giant crater had slowly filled with sediment over billions of years. Their research suggested that much of the sediment was carried into the crater by flowing water. The area seemed like the perfect place to investigate billions of years of Martian history, including the role of water on the planet.

Curiosity was outfitted with a wide array of scientific equipment to help it study the planet. The rover had cameras and radio transmitters so it could communicate with scientists on Earth and send back pictures. It had an arm so it could pick up rocks or dust from the planet's surface. The rover even contained a chemical lab so it could analyze the materials it picked up. The results of the analyses were sent via radio signals to scientists on Earth. Of course, the rover was also mobile. It could roll around the planet's surface to study different parts of the crater. Scientists operated everything remotely from Earth.

Within just a few months of landing, *Curiosity* was already making exciting and important discoveries about the Red Planet. It found a dry, ancient streambed where water once flowed. The stream was probably about knee deep, and water ran through it for thousands of years. After drilling a few inches into the planet's rocky surface, the rover also discovered life-friendly minerals. In combination with water, these minerals suggested that life was possible at some point in Mars's past.

Chapter 7: Space

The next step for *Curiosity* was to find evidence of that life, if it did exist at one time. However, scientists were not searching for fossilized bones or little green Martians. The signs of life they were looking for were much smaller. Realistically, they hoped to find traces of microbial life, such as bacteria or single-celled organisms.

Along with the search for signs of life, *Curiosity's* other purpose was to study the possibility of sending humans to Mars. One risk of space travel is exposure to radiation. Earth's atmosphere blocks much of the harmful radiation that moves through space. Mars has no atmosphere, so *Curiosity* took measurements at the planet's surface. The results showed that exposure to radiation on Mars would be about the same as what astronauts experience on the International Space Station. A crewed mission to Mars would certainly have its risks, but the planet itself is possible for humans to visit.

Name _____

Chapter 7: Space

Answer the questions about *Curiosity in Space.*

1. Write **T** for true or **F** for false next to each statement.

   _____ *Curiosity* was a rocket launched by NASA in November 2011.

   _____ Although *Curiosity* did not find evidence of life on Mars, it did find evidence that life could have existed on Mars in the past.

   _____ *Curiosity* measured levels of radiation on the Martian surface.

   _____ The Bradbury Landing Site was named after the scientist who first discovered the Gale Crater.

2. Why was the Gale Crater chosen as the landing site for *Curiosity*?

   _____

   _____

   _____

3. Which of the following was NOT described as one of *Curiosity's* abilities? Place a check mark on the line of the correct answer.

   _____ picking up rocks from the planet's surface

   _____ transmitting photographs back to Earth

   _____ flying to different areas of the Martian landscape

   _____ drilling into the planet's surface

Name _____

Chapter 7: Space

4. *Curiosity* has a lab onboard that can analyze materials found on Mars. Describe one advantage and one disadvantage to having this lab on the rover.

_____

_____

_____

_____

5. Use information from paragraph 6 to write your own definition of *microbial*.

_____

_____

Do you think sending humans to Mars is a good idea? Why or why not?

_____

_____

_____

_____

_____

_____

Name _____

Chapter 7: Space

> What is it like to be an astronaut?

Out of This World Experience

"All right, everyone, let's settle down a bit," said Mr. Singh, addressing his class of excited eighth graders. "We have Ms. Rebecca Farrow here with us today. Ms. Farrow is an astronaut who is a veteran of three space flights, and she's here to answer your questions." He turned to the woman seated in the chair next to his desk. "Ms. Farrow, we're thrilled to have you here. The kids have been talking about nothing else for days," he confessed.

Ms. Farrow got up and faced the class. "I don't know if I've ever had such anticipation for one of my visits before! I'll do my best to live up to your expectations," she added. "As Mr. Singh mentioned, I've participated in three flights into space. My undergraduate degree is in biology, and I have a PhD in biochemistry. I've been fascinated by space ever since I was a little girl and first learned, during a library story time, that humans had walked on the moon. On my next trip into space, I'll be spending six months on the International Space Station," Ms. Farrow paused and sipped from a glass of water on the desk. "So, tell me—what are your questions about space or being an astronaut?"

Hands quickly shot up across the classroom. Ms. Farrow pointed to a girl in the back of the class with a ponytail. "What should you study in college if you want to be an astronaut?" she asked.

"You should study whatever you most enjoy," responded Ms. Farrow, "because that will make you a passionate and hard worker. There is no one single field of study for astronauts, and in fact, a crew is often made up of people with fairly different backgrounds. It's helpful to have folks with various areas of expertise, so my advice is to study technology, engineering, math, chemistry—whatever field you excel in."

Ms. Farrow smiled as hands eagerly extended back into the air. "What was the most interesting or amazing or surprising part about going into space?" asked Micah Reynolds.

"Walking in space for the first time was one of the greatest, most memorable moments of my life," said Ms. Farrow thoughtfully. "The absolute immensity of space is almost overwhelming," she added, "and the amazing progress that humans have made to send us there makes me enormously proud."

"Do you think that there are other planets with intelligent life?" asked Kristopher.

Chapter 7: Space

"I'm asked that question probably more than any other," replied Ms. Farrow, "although it's one that I obviously have no concrete answer for. The short answer is yes, I do believe that intelligent life exists on other planets. Based on the size of the universe and the vast number of stars, it seems a bit arrogant to me to think that our sun and planet Earth are the only ones that can support life."

Ms. Farrow gestured to a girl near the window, and Lina cleared her throat. "Do you have to go through any special medical tests before you can become an astronaut?" she asked.

Ms. Farrow nodded, "Yes, that's a fairly important part of the process. It would really be quite a crisis if an astronaut had a heart attack in space or suffered a seizure or a stroke. Because access to medical treatment is so limited, NASA does its best to ensure that only people with no serious medical issues travel into space. In addition, the mere fact of being in space is hard on your body. Because of the lack of gravity, you get less blood to your calves and feet. Your bones can lose calcium. Even depression can set in during long missions."

"I'm going to stop you there," said Mr. Singh, waving one hand at the students who groaned. "We can talk a little more with Ms. Farrow following lunch. I like your thoughtful questions," he added. "Just hold on to them for about 45 minutes!"

Spectrum Reading Grade 8

Name _____

Chapter 7: Space

> Answer the questions about *Out of This World Experience*.

1. According to Ms. Farrow, what should you study in college if you want to become an astronaut? Why?

   _____
   _____
   _____

2. Who is the protagonist in this story?

   _____

3. Reread the second line of dialogue in paragraph 6. What does this line tell you about Ms. Farrow?

   _____
   _____
   _____

4. On the lines below, write a summary for paragraph 10.

   _____
   _____
   _____
   _____

Name _____

Chapter 7: Space

5. This selection is written almost as an interview with Ms. Farrow. Did the author's choice of style work for this story? Why or why not?

_____

_____

_____

_____

6. In paragraph 8, Ms. Farrow says, "It seems a bit arrogant to me to think that our sun and planet Earth are the only ones that can support life." What do you think she means by this?

_____

_____

_____

_____

If you were able to ask an astronaut one question, what would it be?

_____

_____

_____

_____

Spectrum Reading Grade 8

Name _____

Chapter 7: Space

Is it possible to grow vegetables on the moon?

Moon Veggies

The next time you go to the grocery store, pick up a zucchini or a red pepper and look at the sticker on it. Where did it come from—California? Chile? What would you think about eating a vegetable that was grown on the moon? This isn't something that we are likely to see soon on supermarket shelves, but NASA is planning to attempt growing several varieties of lunar vegetables. This will be the first life-science experiment performed in what scientists refer to as "deep space." The goal is to show that humans may someday be able to live—and provide food for themselves—on the moon.

In the summer of 2013, six explorers lived in a simulated Mars habitat in Hawaii for four months. One of their goals was to see what the effects were of eating freeze-dried food on a long-term space mission. Although the explorers gave the flavors of the foods fairly high ratings, the first thing they wanted when they left the habitat was fresh fruits and vegetables. Apparently, there is really no satisfying substitute.

In 2015, NASA sent cress (an herb that can be used in salads), basil, and turnip seeds to the moon in specially designed canisters. The seed habitats contained everything the plants needed to grow, including a nutrient-rich paper, enough air in the canisters for 5 to 10 days of growth, and water. The temperature and light in the canisters were regulated. Cameras recorded the growth of the plants, and scientists compared the growth with that of the same seeds grown on Earth.

There is no doubt that the moon has a very different environment than Earth. It has one-sixth the gravity of Earth, as well as harsh radiation from the sun. The side that faces the sun is unbearably hot at about 150° F. On the opposite side of the moon, the temperature is –150° F. These are hardly ideal conditions for creating life, yet the conditions inside the canisters should make it possible.

In addition to their potential to provide food for astronauts, or even future visitors to space, NASA scientists are curious about the plants' ability to grow and thrive in space. Plants need many of the same things humans do to survive—food, water, and air. If plants can survive in deep space, it is one indication that humans may be able to do the same one day. Plants also provide comfort to people in a foreign landscape. In a barren place like the moon, the sight of something green and growing can be a reminder of home. Greenhouses in Antarctica and on the International Space Station have proved popular for these very reasons.

Chapter 7: Space

The planned lunar garden was the first of several experiments that will be performed on the moon. The team working on the project hopes to gradually extend the life the vegetable plants so that they can be observed through various stages of growth, including reproduction.

The habitat will be sent to the moon aboard the Moon Express Lander, a commercial spacecraft that is competing to win a prize by landing on the moon. Even some lucky students will have a chance to try a similar experiment themselves. NASA plans to send materials used to build the plant habitats to schools around the country so that students can try to grow the seeds themselves. And perhaps one day, you'll be able to buy some moon produce in your local grocery store.

Name _____

Chapter 7: Space

Answer the questions about *Moon Veggies*.

1. What foods did explorers in the simulated Mars habitat most miss during their experiment?
   _____

2. Why do you think the seeds will not be planted directly on the moon?
   _____
   _____

3. How is the ability to grow plants on the moon related to the concept of humans someday living on the moon?
   _____
   _____
   _____

4. In what way do plants provide psychological comfort for humans?
   _____
   _____

5. The author's purpose in writing this selection is to
   _____ .

Name _____

Chapter 7: Space

6. What three main elements do the canisters contain?

   _____
   _____
   _____

7. On the lines below, write a summary of paragraph 2.

   _____
   _____
   _____

Make a list of plants you think NASA should try to grow on the moon. Explain your reasons.

_____
_____
_____
_____
_____
_____
_____

Spectrum Reading Grade 8

Name _____

Chapter 7: Space

> Will life on the moon be as lonely as Markus imagines?

Home, Home on the Moon

Looking through the thick, plastic window, Markus watched Earth shrink as the spacecraft carried him farther and farther away from home. My old home, anyway, he thought. He could hardly imagine what living in his new home would be like. His mother had sent videos showing everyone how she had decorated the rooms to be cozy and comfortable, but outside of every window, Markus could see the moon's rocky, desolate landscape stretching away to meet the pitch-black sky.

Markus looked over at his sister, Madison, who sat across the aisle with their father. She looked as grim as he felt. Neither of them had wanted to make the move, but his mother's stay at the colony had been extended for another two years, and their father insisted that they all needed to be together as a family. Markus couldn't wait to see his mother, but leaving Earth was tough. When his friends had thrown a going away party for him, he had acted like he was having fun, but the entire time he was close to breaking down into tears. Markus closed his eyes and tried to picture everything going on as normal—seeing his friends at school, taking piano lessons, being dropped off at swim team practice—but when he opened his eyes, he was still thousands of miles away, moving through the emptiness of space.

The pilot announced that they were just a few minutes away from landing. Everyone onboard sat up and began craning their necks to look out the windows. The spacecraft banked to the left, and Markus got a clear view of the colony spread across the lunar landscape below. He remembered flying in an airplane on Earth. When the plane approached the airport for a landing, you could make out cars, trains, and even people moving around on the ground. As they approached the colony, though, Markus saw nothing moving at all; the place looked lifeless.

The spacecraft touched down on a runway built across the moon's surface and entered the colony through huge doors that immediately shut behind them once they were inside. Loud whooshing sounds surrounded them as oxygen was pumped into the space where the craft now sat. When the sound suddenly ceased, the pilot announced that it was time to exit the craft. Markus, Madison, and their father headed down the aisle to the spacecraft's exit, walked across a small bridge, and went through a door that took them into the heart of the colony.

Name _____

Chapter 7: Space

It was a massive, open room with people hurrying about or standing in small groups talking. The place reminded Markus of a mall, with planters filled with greenery, escalators carrying people to different levels, and seating scattered throughout. High overhead, a domed, glass ceiling covered the entire area, but instead of a blue sky, Markus saw the blackness of space through it. Then, he noticed Earth, which hung like a brilliant blue-green jewel amid all that emptiness.

Markus's mother wasn't there to meet them—she was busy working on her research assignment—but they would see her that evening. In the meantime, they headed to the cafeteria to get something to eat.

As Markus stood in line, someone tapped him on the shoulder and said, "Hey, Markus! Welcome to the space place."

Markus turned around and exclaimed, "Isabella! I haven't seen you since sixth grade. Is this where you went?"

"Yeah, we've been here a couple of years now," Isabella explained. "I heard you were coming up here—word gets around in a place like this—and I remember how much I hated it at first. I wanted to be sure to say hi as soon as you got here. After classes tomorrow, I'll show you the ropes."

And for the first time in nearly a month, Markus smiled.

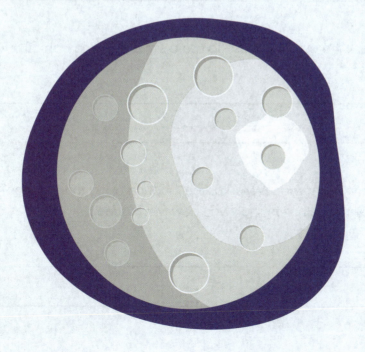

Spectrum Reading Grade 8

Name _____

Chapter 7: Space

> Answer the questions about *Home, Home on the Moon.*

1. Write a short paragraph summarizing the plot of the story.

   _____
   _____
   _____

2. Identify two aspects of the story that are fantasy.

   _____
   _____
   _____

3. Identify two aspects of the story that are realistic.

   _____
   _____
   _____

4. Why do you think the author choose to use a simile in paragraph 5?

   _____
   _____
   _____

5. For most of the story, how does Markus feel about moving to the moon? Identify words or phrases used by the author to show you how Markus feels.

   _____
   _____

Name _____

Chapter 7: Space

6. How does Markus feel about the move at the end of the story? How does the author show you Markus's feelings at the end?

_____

_____

_____

7. What does the main area inside the colony remind Markus of? Place a check mark on the line of the correct answer.

_____ an airport

_____ a mall

_____ an office building

_____ a cafeteria

Describe a time when you were new to a place or an activity and someone helped you feel more comfortable.

_____

_____

_____

_____

Spectrum Reading Grade 8

Chapter 8: Under Water

Before Reading

Get your student ready to read with before-reading prompts and exercises.

- What do you already know about ocean explorers?
- What is a memorable experience you've had at the ocean?
- Skim through the pages of this chapter. Look at the titles of the selections, illustrations and/or photographs, italicized words, and any other text features.
- Make predictions. What do you think you will read about in this chapter?

During Reading

Encourage your student to use close-reading strategies to gain a deeper understanding of the text.

- Create a timeline of events from a fictional story.
- Number the paragraphs in the margin to use when analyzing text and providing evidence.
- Try and identify any opinions the author of the selection has. Do you agree with their opinions?

After Reading

Your student should complete the page(s) of questions following each selection to demonstrate their comprehension of the text. Support their reading comprehension with after-reading reflection questions.

- Were your predictions correct?
- What did you learn?
- How did you connect to the text?

Helpful Definitions

Having a good grasp of the vocabulary found in a reading selection is key for reading comprehension. Before reading each definition, ask your student: *What do you think this word means? Is there another word you know that has the same root? Does the part of speech help you understand the word's meaning?*

dissertation: an extensive written piece about a topic, usually for an academic degree

vital: very important or essential

venues: places where events are held

untethered: freed from

submersible: small underwater craft

hauled: pulled or dragged something heavy

demand: urgent need

endurance: the ability to do something difficult for a long time

inspiration: something that inspires someone, such as a person, an event, or an idea

persevere: to continue to do or try to do something, even if you have difficulties or are unlikely to succeed

decompression: the act of releasing pressure

Name _____

Chapter 8: Under Water

What inspires oceanographer and marine biologist Sylvia Earle?

The Sturgeon General

Sylvia Earle has had a fascination with the sea ever since she was a little girl. She grew up on a small New Jersey farm, and first encountered the ocean on a trip to the beach when she was three. Earle's family moved to Florida when she was 12, and the Gulf of Mexico became her new backyard. Earle's interest in and love for the ocean began in earnest then. She was never scared of the ocean or fearful of its creatures. Instead, Earle was mesmerized by its beauty and respectful of the animals that made their home there.

Earle's parents could not afford to pay her tuition for college, but she was an accomplished student and earned a scholarship to Florida State. Earle paid for the remainder of her tuition by working in laboratories while she was in school. Earle completed her bachelor's degree in science in 1955, and over the next 11 years, earned her master's degree and PhD while also marrying and starting a family.

Earle's dissertation for her PhD was an in-depth exploration and study of aquatic plant life in the Gulf of Mexico. No scientist had ever done that kind of detailed study of ocean vegetation before, and Earle received much admiration for her work. To her, plants are a vital part of the oceans and the first step in understanding the complex ecosystems below the sea.

Earle's career and study of the ocean continued in a variety of venues. In 1969, Earle applied for the Tektite project. She wanted to be one of the scientists chosen to live for several weeks in an enclosed habitat on the ocean floor. Despite her experience, Earle was not chosen, at least in part because the overseers of the project did not think that men and women should live together in such close quarters. A year later, Earle led a team of all female scientists on another Tektite mission, 50 feet below the ocean's surface. This expedition increased Earle's visibility as a scientist and oceanographer. To Earle, anything that brought the public's attention to the oceans was a good thing.

Over the next decade, Earle traveled all over the world, visiting and exploring the waters around the Galápagos Islands, China, the Bahamas, and the Indian Ocean. Earle began working with an undersea photographer named Al Giddings. She and Giddings decided to make a documentary about sperm whales. The two followed whales in their journeys through the world's oceans. Once again, Earle was able to bring the oceans to people at home. She believed that it was hard to care about something you don't know about. Earle considered it her job to bring that knowledge to as many people as possible.

Name _____

Chapter 8: Under Water

    In 1979, Earle set a record for walking untethered on the ocean floor at a greater depth than any other human being had. She wore something called a Jim suit, which looked a bit like an astronaut's space gear. For more than two hours, Earle explored the ocean floor at a depth of 1,250 feet. She was attached by a communication line to the nearby submersible, but nothing connected her to the world above the ocean. Even more than 45 years later, no one has broken Earle's record.

    In 2009, Earle founded Mission Blue, a program that has identified over 140 places around the world to protect marine biodiversity. Today, Earle is an Explorer-in-Residence for the National Geographic Society. She has spent approximately 7,000 hours underwater, yet the ocean still holds the same attraction for her. In an effort to raise awareness about the ocean and its importance to all life on Earth, she led a climate expedition to Antarctica in 2023 and has more trips planned for the future. Earle, who was named Time magazine's first "Hero of the Planet," has referred to the world's oceans as our planet's "blue heart." She believes that in order to keep our planet healthy and alive, we must care for its heart.

Spectrum Reading Grade 8

Name _____

Chapter 8: Under Water

> Answer the questions about *The Sturgeon General*.

1. Sylvia Earle has had a(n) _____ fascination with the world's oceans.

    _____ temporary

    _____ everlasting

    _____ remote

2. Earle has always worked to increase the public's _____ of the importance of the oceans.

    _____ awareness

    _____ visibility

    _____ perception

3. Write three character traits that describe Sylvia Earle. Provide text evidence to support each trait.

    _____

    _____

    _____

4. On the lines below, write the main idea of the selection.

    _____

    _____

    _____

Name _____

Chapter 8: Under Water

5. Which word or words best describe the selection?

   _____ historical fiction

   _____ biography

   _____ persuasive essay

6. What was the topic of the documentary Earle and Giddings made together?
   _____

7. According to Earle, what is the "blue heart," and why is it important?
   _____
   _____
   _____
   _____
   _____
   _____
   _____

Spectrum Reading Grade 8

Name _____

Chapter 8: Under Water

> Will a change in attitude make a difference in the livelihood of the Dunkirk family?

Fishing for Change

Fiona's dad handed her a cup of steaming coffee from his thermos. Fiona wrapped her hand around her mug and watched the steam dance up into the watercolor blue morning sky. The water lapped gently against the boat, and Fiona smiled, remembering being rocked to sleep by the waves for dozens of long-ago naps.

"I'm trying to remember the last time we did this, just the two of us," wondered Mr. Dunkirk. He adjusted his hat and leaned back for a moment, inhaling deeply. "I've been coming out here practically every day since I was 16," he added, "and I still never get tired of the ocean air."

"What are we trying to bring in today, Dad?" asked Fiona, standing up and stretching.

"Hold on just a minute, and I'll show you," responded Mr. Dunkirk. He hauled in a small net, and a moment later there was a mess of flopping, wriggling dogfish on the boat's deck.

Fiona laughed and gave her dad a searching look. "If I'm remembering correctly, and I'm pretty sure I am, you always said that dogfish was garbage fish, not worth even the fuel it costs to haul it in."

Fiona's dad grinned and clapped her on the shoulder. "I'm impressed that you were listening to all my words of wisdom out here, Fiona, but times are changing, and if I want to preserve the family tradition, I need to change too."

Mr. Dunkirk proceeded to tell his daughter how hard things had actually been for the past few years. Fiona acted as though it was all news to her, but the truth was that she had overheard some of her parents' hushed and worried conversations after they thought she was sleeping. And anyway, it was hard to live in a New England fishing village, surrounded by people who made their living from the ocean, without knowing that times were hard.

The fish that had supported the Dunkirk family for the past four generations were no longer available in the quantities that they used to be. Some of the problem had to do with new government regulations, but Fiona knew that overfishing of popular species was also an issue. She had heard some people complaining that it was ridiculous that you couldn't even find local cod in Cape Cod anymore.

Chapter 8: Under Water

"So how is dogfish going to change all this for us?" asked Fiona, staring with new interest at the large spotted creatures.

"It all started with Nico Kovitch," began Mr. Dunkirk, "who opened that new restaurant out by the pier. His focus is on fresh, local, and sustainable, and his customers can't get enough of it—he's got lines out the door most nights."

Fiona's dad continued excitedly with his story. Chef Kovitch had been traveling in Europe and had tried cape shark (more commonly known as dogfish) at a restaurant. He loved the mild, creamy flavor and talked to the chef at the restaurant about his sources for the fish.

"Chef Kovitch couldn't believe that the dogfish came from what is essentially his own backyard!" exclaimed Mr. Dunkirk. "These dogfish we've been throwing back are getting all kinds of new attention here," he added. "They're plentiful, tasty, and according to the chef, they're easy to cook. Apparently, calling them dogfish isn't adding to their appeal, so on menus, they're referred to as 'cape shark'."

"This is amazing, Dad," replied Fiona. "Are the prices of dogfish going up since there's more of a demand?"

Her dad nodded as he grabbed the old, well-seasoned cast iron pan from its hook. He lit the flame under the small camp stove he kept on the boat. "Want to try some of the fish that's going to turn things around for the Dunkirks?" he added.

"Who could pass that up?" responded Fiona. "It's been a while since I had fish for breakfast!"

Spectrum Reading Grade 8

Name _____

Chapter 8: Under Water

Answer the questions about *Fishing for Change.*

1. How is dogfish regarded differently in Europe than in the United States?
   _____
   _____

2. Explain why the price of dogfish is going up in the story.
   _____
   _____
   _____

3. How would you characterize Fiona's relationship with her dad?
   _____
   _____
   _____

4. Why are chefs calling dogfish "cape shark"?
   _____
   _____

Name _____

Chapter 8: Under Water

5. Fiona knew that her family had been having hard times before her dad told her on the boat. Is this statement true or false?

   _____

6. Explain why the price of dogfish is going up in the story.

   _____

   _____

   _____

7. Which word best describes Mr. Dunkirk's attitude at the end of the story?

   _____ pessimistic

   _____ optimistic

   _____ independent

Do you think that Fiona will follow in the family tradition of fishing for a living when she grows up? Why or why not?

_____

_____

_____

_____

Name _____

Chapter 8: Under Water

How do distance swimmers prepare for races?

Going the Distance

Vijay spotted Cameron in the hallway of Garfield Heights High School. "Hey, Cam, I heard you're training for a marathon. When is it? I might want to compete too."

Cameron appeared confused for a minute and then laughed. "Oh, I know what you mean! Actually, I'm a marathon swimmer. Marathon, or distance, swimmers complete races that are longer than most aquatic competitions held in pools, although distance competitions are sometimes held in pools."

"Are you swimming the English Channel or something?" Vijay asked.

"No, that's way out of my league at this point—this marathon I'm going to be competing in is a 10-kilometer race in Sandusky Bay a few months from now. It'll take me a few more months of training to become a competitive swimmer for this race. I've competed five-kilometer races in the past, but this competition will require a lot more endurance than the races I'm used to," Cameron explained, expertly twirling the dial on his locker.

"How long will the entire race take then?" asked Vijay.

Cameron grabbed an algebra textbook from his locker and shut the door. "I'll be in the water for a little over three hours, but it's not like I'll be in the middle of the ocean. I'm swimming in a loop race, which means I'll swim in Sandusky Bay, but I'll be swimming in circles that return to a boat every thirty minutes or so. I can get water for hydration during the race, or even a small snack when I need it—kind of the way marathon runners do."

"Distance swimming sounds pretty intense," Vijay said. "I think I may be more of a runner. Do you wear regular swim trunks or is there some kind of special wet suit or something?"

"It depends," replied Cameron, "because the rules are different for different racing organizations. A lot of people think distance swimmers shouldn't wear compression swimsuits, although personally they make me feel more comfortable. Honestly, I think they make me a little faster too. This upcoming race, the Great Sandusky Swim, allows them, so that's what I'll wear. I also like to wear a swimming cap with a chinstrap, but I won't be able to wear one in this race, which bans caps with straps. I'll also wear goggles, earplugs, and a nose clip. I'll use a skin lubricant, too, to help keep my body from chafing, to keep me a little warmer, and to ward off jellyfish stings," Cameron added.

Chapter 8: Under Water

"Jellyfish stings!" exclaimed Vijay. "In Lake Erie—are you serious?"

Cameron nodded. "Isn't that extremely weird? I always thought that jellyfish only lived in the oceans, but there are actually small, freshwater jellyfish in the Great Lakes."

"That's another good reason for me to stick to running!" exclaimed Vijay, as the boys headed down the hallway to their algebra class. "How are you training for the race?" Vijay asked.

"I've been increasing the length of my swims by one-kilometer increments," Cameron replied. "A five-kilometer race has become almost easy, so I've worked up to an eight-kilometer swim. I don't do the longer distances every week, but I consistently swim at least five kilometers each week, completing longer races every other week. The most important thing is for me to be consistent in my training, which is really building my endurance—I haven't become exhausted during any swim yet. Do you think you'd want to train for the next race with me?"

The sound of the bell echoed shrilly through the hallway as Cameron and Vijay reached their classroom. "Ah, saved by the bell," Vijay joked. "I'm not so sure that distance swimming is for me, but I'd give it a try," he said. "Maybe you hit the streets with me for a run now and then, and I'll see if I can muster up the courage to battle the Lake Erie jellyfish."

Spectrum Reading Grade 8

Name _____

Chapter 8: Under Water

> Answer the questions about *Going the Distance*.

1. How are running a marathon and swimming a marathon similar?

   _____
   _____
   _____

2. Why does Cameron wear a skin lubricant during a distance race?

   _____
   _____
   _____

3. Based on the selection, what are three character traits you could use to describe Cameron?

   _____
   _____
   _____

4. Vijay is surprised to hear that _____ live in Lake Erie.

   _____ jellyfish

   _____ sharks

   _____ stingrays

150 Spectrum Reading Grade 8

Name _____

Chapter 8: Under Water

5. Sometimes, authors have more than one purpose in writing. For this story, entertainment is one purpose. What is the other?

   _____

6. Do you think that Vijay will train for a long-distance swimming competition with Cameron next time? Explain.

   _____

   _____

   _____

Have you ever participated in any kind of race? If you have, describe your experience. If you haven't, explain why you would or would not like to compete in a race in the future.

_____

_____

_____

_____

_____

_____

_____

Spectrum Reading **Grade 8**

Name _____

Chapter 8: Under Water

> How did one long distance swimmer have the willpower to complete a record-setting swim?

Find a Way

Long distance swimmer Diana Nyad is nearly unstoppable. At the age of 64, she set a record for a swim she attempted four other times, beginning when she was 28 years old. Nyad wanted to show the world that you can always find a way to follow your dreams. She also wanted to send the message that you are never too old to reach your goals. Diana Nyad captured the attention and hearts of people around the world. People rooted her on, knowing that enormous personal strength and endurance allowed Nyad to keep going when others might have quit.

Nyad first caught the public's attention in 1975, when she swam around Manhattan Island, a distance of 28 miles, in slightly under 8 hours. She first attempted the swim from Havana, Cuba, to Key West, Florida, three years later, at the age of 28. During this attempt, she swam inside a steel shark cage. She completed 42 hours of the swim but had to quit because large waves kept slamming her into the shark cage and were throwing her well off course.

Although Nyad continued swimming, she did not attempt the swim from Cuba to Florida again for another 33 years. In 2011, Nyad attempted the swim, this time without a protective shark cage. Again, strong currents threw Nyad off course, but the main factor in her decision to quit this time was a flare-up of asthma. Nyad had to continually flip onto her back to catch her breath. Eleven hours into her asthma attack, Nyad knew that she wasn't going to make it.

At this point, many people would have given up, but Nyad was determined to reach her goal and complete the 110-mile swim. Just about six weeks following her second attempt, Nyad tried again. Although she completed about two-thirds of the total distance, she was unable to finish because of severe jellyfish and Portuguese man-of-war stings. Afterwards, Nyad reported that she had never been in so much pain. Her face was red and swollen, and some of the man-of-war stings had temporarily paralyzed muscles in her back.

Still determined to beat her greatest challenge, Nyad set out on her fourth attempt in August of 2012. Although she wore a nylon bodysuit to protect her from jellyfish stings, she was stung repeatedly on her lips where the suit had an opening. Large sharks circled below her. Nyad was not swimming in a shark cage, and although her team was using an electronic shark repellant, there were no guarantees that the system was foolproof. Thunderstorms and lightning threatened Nyad's safety and that of her crew. She decided it wasn't worth putting everyone at risk of a lightning strike, and so Nyad's fourth attempt also ended without success.

Chapter 8: Under Water

In August of 2013, Diana Nyad began her fifth and final attempt at swimming from Cuba to Florida across the Florida Straits. Once again, she did not swim in a shark cage, but her team of 35 did keep a lookout for sharks, as well as use the electronic repellant. She wore a full body suit, a mask, gloves, and booties to protect her body from jellyfish stings. Fifty-three hours and 110 miles later, Nyad walked onto the shores of Florida, amid cheers of fans and well-wishers.

Nyad was 64 years old when she completed her swim—an age at which many people are retiring and starting to take it easy in life. Nyad battled wind and rough currents on her trip. She vomited from having too much salt water in her body. The night before the last leg of her swim, Nyad's team didn't stop to feed her because she was so cold, they felt it was more important for her to keep swimming to try to stay warm.

Today, Nyad uses her experiences to give inspirational talks. She hopes that in some way her journey will serve as an inspiration to others to persevere, to follow their dreams, and to find a way.

Spectrum Reading Grade 8

Name _____

Chapter 8: Under Water

Answer the questions about *Find a Way*.

1. What were Nyad's greatest problems during her attempted swims across the Florida Straits?

   _____

   _____

2. Between which two places did Nyad attempt to swim four times before she was successful?

   _____

3. Why do you think Nyad chose not to use the shark cage after her first attempt?

   _____

   _____

   _____

4. What are two of the messages Nyad wanted to communicate to people through her swimming?

   _____

   _____

   _____

   _____

Name _____

Chapter 8: Under Water

5. What three adjectives could you use to describe Diana Nyad?

   _____

   _____

   _____

6. What sort of protective equipment did Nyad use during her swims?

   _____

   _____

   _____

7. Do you think that athletic heroes like Nyad are a useful inspiration to everyday people? Why or why not?

   _____

   _____

   _____

> Write about an experience you've had when you wished you could quit but instead you kept going.
>
> _____
>
> _____
>
> _____
>
> _____

Spectrum Reading Grade 8

Name _____

Chapter 8: Under Water

What would it be like to live and work underwater?

The Age of Aquarius

Imagine living and working deep in the ocean. For some people, this idea might sound a little frightening. Others are fascinated by the chance to experience a mysterious world that so few humans get to see firsthand. Aquarius Reef Base is an undersea laboratory and habitat located about 5.4 miles off the coast of Key Largo, Florida. It sits in a sandy area near a coral reef, about 60 feet below the ocean's surface.

Aquarius is owned and operated by Florida International University. Scientists live in Aquarius for about 10 days at a time. There, they have the chance to spend 8 hours a day in the ocean without having to return to the surface. Aquarius is equipped with many comforts of home. It has six bunk beds, a shower, a toilet, a microwave, a refrigerator, computers, and Internet connection. The vessel measures about 43 feet long and 9 feet wide. Since 1993, more than 150 missions have been completed on Aquarius!

One of the greatest benefits to scientists working in Aquarius (often known as "aquanauts") is that they do not need to surface regularly the way scuba divers do. Decompression sickness is always a risk to scuba divers. Also known as "the bends," it is the result of the pressure differences deep underwater and at the surface. Common symptoms are joint pain, rashes, headaches, and dizziness. In severe cases, it can result in death. Aquanauts do not need to surface after a dive. They just return to Aquarius, which is pressurized. At the end of a mission, the scientists spend about 17 hours undergoing decompression. The pressure in Aquarius is slowly reduced over that time, so that the scientists can return to the surface without any ill effects.

The goal of the undersea explorers who work and live in Aquarius are diverse. The one thing they have in common is the desire to learn about and protect the oceans. Aquarius's nearness to a coral reef offers scientists an up-close look at this amazing habitat. Coral reefs around the world are threatened by pollution, overfishing, and climate change. Scientists can perform experiments, record observations, and take samples that allow them to better understand the reefs and their role in underwater ecosystems. In addition, they can determine the ways that humans can best protect the reefs and save them from more damage.

Name _____

Chapter 8: Under Water

One example of research done on Aquarius involves looking at the effects of UV rays on coral. Coral produces a chemical that protects it from UV rays. This is similar to the way sunblock protects humans. A decrease in the ozone layer, the result of pollution, is causing UV rays to become more intense. This means that a coral reef's natural protection is no longer as effective as it once was.

Going forward, Florida International University hopes to offer more educational opportunities via Aquarius. What better way to create enthusiasm and a sense of responsibility for the oceans than to allow students to closely observe what is at risk? Classes are already sometimes taught in real time from Aquarius. There are several observation windows, so a simple Internet connection can allow students the experience of watching the undersea activities around the lab.

Spectrum Reading Grade 8

Name _____

Chapter 8: Under Water

Answer the questions about *The Age of Aquarius.*

1. Find the word in each paragraph that matches the definition.

   an assignment, task, or job (in paragraph 3)

   _____

   systems made up of living things that interact with each other and their environment (in paragraph 4)

   _____

   a lessening (in paragraph 5)

   _____

2. What causes "the bends"?

   _____
   _____
   _____

3. Aquarius is currently located off the coast of _____ .

Name _____

Chapter 8: Under Water

4. What kind of research can aquanauts do on the nearby coral reef?

   _____
   _____
   _____
   _____

Would you enjoy spending time in an undersea research station like Aquarius? Why or why not?

_____
_____
_____
_____
_____
_____
_____

Name _____

Chapter 8: Under Water

> What motivates Dylan to swim farther than he has ever swum before?

Every Lap Counts

The muscles in Dylan's arms and legs burned, and with each breath, he wondered if he should be done, but as he touched the wall at the end of the pool, he automatically turned for another lap. *I can do one more*, Dylan told himself. *This is for Charley*. He was starting his seventh lap—farther than he had ever swum before—and he was definitely feeling the effort.

As Dylan's head moved in and out of the water, he heard cheering and clapping echoing through the tiled space, first muffled, then clear, and then muffled again as water covered his ears. In the next lane, he caught a glimpse of his teammate, Kaitlyn, splashing along in the opposite direction. Dylan wondered how many laps she had completed so far. He normally felt competitive toward the other swimmers, but today he hoped she swam more laps than anyone else.

Dylan passed below the banner that stretched overhead, spanning from one side of the room to the other above the center of the pool. In big red letters, the banner announced, *Swim for Charley! Every Lap Counts!* Dylan and the other members of his swim team were taking part in a swimathon to raise money for Dylan's best friend, Charley Watkins. Earlier in the year, Charley had been diagnosed with multiple sclerosis. He needed physical therapy and expensive medications. After Charley's friends learned of the medical burden on Charley's family, they started brainstorming ways to help. Several of Charley's friends were on the swim team, so that led to the idea of a swimathon.

For a month, Dylan and the other swim team members had asked for pledges from anyone who would help: family members, friends, and neighbors. Most people pledged a dollar or two per lap, but others were amazingly generous. Dylan's grandmother offered to donate $10 for each lap Dylan swam! Considering the number of pledges the team had received altogether, and with each team member swimming at least four or five laps, they figured they would raise more than $1,000.

Dylan touched the wall again and spun around to head down the length of the pool for the eighth time. Even though the chlorine stung his eyes, he noticed that his muscles felt looser and no longer ached. *I'm getting my second wind*, Dylan thought. His instinct was to begin swimming faster, but he knew that would be a mistake. He wasn't in a race—the goal was to swim as long as possible—so he held back and paced himself.

Name _____

Chapter 8: Under Water

Finally, as Dylan completed his tenth lap, he knew he was too exhausted to keep going. *If I try another lap, I'll end up treading water in the middle of the pool, waiting for someone to come get me*, he thought. Dylan pulled himself up onto the edge of the pool and sat panting for a couple of minutes, quietly resting before he tried to stand.

Dylan's father approached him and placed a towel around his shoulders. "Wow, Dylan," his father said, shaking his head in amazement. "I am so impressed. You were obviously motivated, because that's farther than anyone else has swum today, and I know it's farther than you've ever swum before."

Dylan stood, feeling the wobbliness of his legs, and slowly walked with his father back to the benches where the other swimmers sat alongside Charley. Coach Templeton smiled and congratulated Dylan on his hard work, and then Charley rose and bumped fists with Dylan.

"My parents and I are giving a 'thank you' speech to everyone at the potluck afterward," Charley told his friend, "but you deserve one now. Thanks, Dude."

"Naw," Dylan insisted, "it's no big deal. I know you'd do the same for me. So, when do we eat? I'm starving." And the two friends laughed.

Spectrum Reading Grade 8

Name _____

Chapter 8: Under Water

Answer the questions about *Every Lap Counts*.

1. Why are the students having a swimathon?

   _____

   _____

2. How many laps did Dylan complete?

   _____

3. Even though his arms and legs ache, Dylan keeps swimming. What does this tell you about his character?

   _____

   _____

4. Which of the following would NOT be considered as one of the themes of this story?

   _____ generosity

   _____ friendship

   _____ competitiveness

   _____ teamwork

5. This story was told using third-person limited point of view, which means the story was told by a narrator, but mainly from the perspective of one character. Which character's perspective was used for telling the story?

   _____

Name _____

Chapter 8: Under Water

6. Choose one of the other characters and explain how the story would be different it were told from that character's perspective.

_____

_____

_____

_____

7. Authors include sensory details to make their stories more interesting. Sensory details describe sights, sounds, smells, tastes, and textures experienced by the characters. Find examples in the text of details describing three different senses. Record the senses and examples below.

Sense: _____ Example: _____

Sense: _____ Example: _____

Sense: _____ Example: _____

Why is it important for friends to help each other in times of trouble? Provide a personal example as part of your answer.

_____

_____

_____

_____

Spectrum Reading Grade 8

Chapter 8: Under Water

> How would you describe the dark side of oceans?

The Ocean
by Nathaniel Hawthorne

The Ocean has its silent caves,
Deep, quiet, and alone;
Though there be fury on the waves,
Beneath them there is none.
The awful spirits of the deep
Hold their communion there;
And there are those for whom we weep,
The young, the bright, the fair.

Calmly the wearied seamen rest
Beneath their own blue sea.
The ocean solitudes are blest,
For there is purity.
The earth has guilt, the earth has care,
Unquiet are its graves;
But peaceful sleep is ever there,
Beneath the dark blue waves.

Name _____

Chapter 8: Under Water

Answer the questions about "The Ocean."

1. What is the message of the poem?

   _____
   _____

2. What is the mood of the poem?

   _____
   _____

3. How does the author develop this mood?

   _____
   _____
   _____

> Try rewriting a few lines of the poem with alternative words that would change the mood of the original poem.
>
> _____
> _____
> _____
> _____

Spectrum Reading Grade 8

Chapter 9: Bees

Before Reading

Get your student ready to read with before-reading prompts and exercises.

- What do you already know about bees?
- What do you want to learn about bees?
- Skim through the pages of this chapter. Look at the titles of the selections, illustrations and/or photographs, italicized words, and any other text features.
- Make predictions. What do you think you will read about in this chapter?

During Reading

Encourage your student to use close-reading strategies to gain a deeper understanding of the text.

- Take notes while reading.
- Think about what would have been another good illustration or photo for the selection as you read.
- How is the selection you are reading organized? Could it have been organized in a different way?
- Think about any information you think is missing from the selection.

After Reading

Your student should complete the page(s) of questions following each selection to demonstrate their comprehension of the text. Support their reading comprehension with after-reading reflection questions.

- Were your predictions correct?
- What did you learn?
- How did you connect to the text?

Helpful Definitions

Having a good grasp of the vocabulary found in a reading selection is key for reading comprehension. Before reading each definition, ask your student: *What do you think this word means? Is there another word you know that has the same root? Does the part of speech help you understand the word's meaning?*

rigamarole: something (such as a procedure or an explanation) that is long, complicated, and tedious

crystallize: to cause to form crystals

embalming: treating a dead body to protect it from decay

remedy: a medicine or treatment that relieves or cures a disease

humectant: a substance that promotes retention of moisture

slender: small or narrow

Name _____

Chapter 9: Bees

What kinds of information do you need to have before you get your own beehive?

Honey Hill Farm

Dani and her dad sat on a faded quilt with a dozen other future beekeepers. It was an early spring day, and the morning air was still crisp. Several bees buzzed busily around the hive, while Mr. Loughton, the beekeeper, chatted with a young couple.

The previous fall, Dani had written a research paper about bees and their recently declining populations. Before that, she'd never thought much about bees, aside from trying to avoid them when she was barefoot. One article she'd read discussed the responsibility of everyday people in making global change. Raising bees seemed like recycling to Dani—it was a small thing she could do to make a difference. And her dad was always on board with new ideas for things they could do or make themselves, especially if they were good for your health or the planet.

"All right, folks," began Mr. Loughton, "I'd like to give you some basic information about beekeeping so that you feel comfortable when your bees arrive. I'm hoping that everyone ordered their bees back in January, right?" Everyone nodded, and Mr. Loughton continued. "Good, then let's talk about your options for hives."

Mr. Loughton went on to describe the Langstroth hive—the type of hive he kept on the farm and the one that he said most beekeepers would recommend. Dani recognized the stacks of boxes that looked almost like filing cabinets oddly placed in the middle of a field. In the Langstroth hive, each of the boxes contained a frame where the bees built their honeycomb and stored their honey. You could pull the boxes out like drawers, which gave you easy access to the bees and their honey.

"The extra parts are a bit bulky to store, and the boxes can be heavy to lift," admitted Mr. Loughton. "When you access the hive, you do disrupt the bees, which means that you may want to have a smoker on hand to calm them."

"The other main hive system, the top bar hive, is less disruptive to the bees and is lighter to work with, but you may lose your hive in a cold winter. In addition, I've found in the past that proper ventilation can be a problem."

"I think we should go with the Langstroth hive, don't you?" Mr. Hwang whispered in Dani's ear. Dani nodded in agreement. The reading she'd done so far indicated that supplies and advice about Langstroth hives were also easier to find.

Chapter 9: Bees

"At the same time you order your hive," said Mr. Loughton, "you'll also want to purchase your protective clothing. The veil and gloves are the most important items to purchase, although if you are a beginner and are working with a Langstroth hive, you may want the full-body suit. Some folks also feel that wearing long sleeves and pants, along with the veil and gloves, is sufficient."

Mr. Loughton produced a full-body bee suit, veil, and gloves from a box at his feet. "I also recommend buying a smoker, which is especially helpful for beginner beekeepers. You load it with pine straw or grass, and it produces a thick smoke, which calms the bees and reduces your chances of getting stung. You will get stung, though, by the way," he added, grinning.

Dani noticed a picnic basket sitting on the ground and was about to ask her dad what he thought was inside, when Mr. Loughton picked it up and began passing out biscuits and honey. "I thought you might all be ready for a break," he said, passing out a stack of yellow gingham napkins. "You can sample some of my honey and see if all this rigmarole is worth the effort."

Dani sat back and drizzled the sweet amber honey onto the biscuit. She looked up at the startlingly blue sky and listened to the buzz of the bees as she bit into her biscuit. Oh yeah, she was sure it would be worth it.

Name _____

Chapter 9: Bees

Answer the questions about *Honey Hill Farm*.

1. Name a pro and a con for each of the hive types mentioned in the selection.

Type	Pro	Con

2. The purpose of a smoker is to

   _____ cause the bees to produce more honey.

   _____ calm the bees.

   _____ encourage the queen to lay more eggs.

3. What character traits does Mr. Loughton have? Describe how they affect his role as a teacher of beekeeping.

   _____

   _____

   _____

   _____

Name _____

Chapter 9: Bees

4. Do you think that the beekeeping class is giving Dani and Mr. Hwang a realistic idea of what beekeeping is like? Why or why not?

_____

_____

_____

_____

5. Which type of hive would be best suited for a beekeeper in a northern state?

_____

6. What two purposes do you think the author had for writing this story?

_____

_____

_____

_____

Is beekeeping a hobby that appeals to you? Why or why not?

_____

_____

_____

Spectrum Reading Grade 8

Name _____

Chapter 9: Bees

What are some of the many uses for honey?

Sweet as Honey

Honey is a sweet treat that most people take for granted. It appears on grocery store shelves, often in a cute plastic bear squeeze bottle. If you're lucky, your local farmers' market may even carry fresh honey, brought to you directly by the beekeeper. But honey is more than just a topping for waffles or a sweetener for tea. It's a miracle of sorts.

Have you ever consumed anything made by an insect? If you've had honey, then you have! Even with all our technical abilities—sending humans into space, designing computers, creating 3-D printers—no one has figured out how to make artificial honey. There's really no substitute for what bees have always known how to do.

A beehive may contain as many as 60,000 bees. The worker bees, the ones that gather nectar, may visit up to two million flowers just to make a single pound of honey. No wonder some people call it liquid gold! Although amber-colored clover honey tends to be most common, honey comes in a variety of shades and flavors. Honey can be almost clear and have a very mild flavor. It can also be yellow, orange, amber, or almost brown. In general, the lighter honeys have a milder flavor, while the darker honeys have a stronger, bolder flavor. The flavor is influenced by the flower that produced the nectar that the bees used to make the honey. In America, you can buy about 300 different types of honey! Some well-known varieties are alfalfa, clover, orange blossom, sage, eucalyptus, and tupelo.

Honey has been used throughout history in a number of ways. One of the most remarkable things about it is that it never spoils. It may crystallize, meaning that it becomes solid in parts, but simply warming it slightly will melt the crystals and return the honey to its liquid form.

No one knows exactly how long honey has been used by humans, but Spanish cave paintings dated at 7000 BCE show early evidence of beekeeping. Honey was also used by the ancient Egyptians as a sweetener, as a gift to the gods, and even as an element in embalming fluid used to create mummies. Honey has been found inside the Egyptian pyramids, and although that honey was more than 3,000 years old, you could dip your finger in it and take a lick. It would still taste like honey, and it would still be safe to eat. No other food has such lasting power!

Name _____

Chapter 9: Bees

In addition to its many uses as a sweetener, honey has been used for centuries as a medicinal remedy. Because it's very difficult for any kind of bacteria to survive in honey, it makes a perfect barrier on cuts and can prevent infection. Honey is also an effective remedy to soothe a sore throat. It has even been found to be effective in suppressing coughs.

Another use for this remarkable natural substance is in skin and hair products. People have long known that honey is a humectant, which means that it attracts and retains moisture, in addition to being antimicrobial. This makes it a perfect ingredient in lotions, soaps, lip balms, and shampoos. You can purchase many personal products containing honey, or you can try your hand at making your own. Many recipes are available online, and some are as simple as blending two ingredients, such as honey and olive oil, to make a deep conditioning treatment for your hair.

The next time a bee buzzes through your garden or you drizzle some honey on a piece of toast, think about the miracle of honey. It's one of the most perfect foods on the planet—completely natural, made in exactly the same way for millions of years.

Spectrum Reading Grade 8

Name _____

Chapter 9: Bees

Answer the questions about *Sweet as Honey.*

1. How does the author of this selection feel about honey? Support your answer with examples from the selection.

   _____
   _____
   _____
   _____

2. In the selection, what example does the author give of how you can make your own hair product?

   _____
   _____

3. Honey is one of the foods that humans eat that is made by an

   _____ .

4. Give two examples of how honey was used in ancient times.

   _____
   _____
   _____
   _____

Name _____

Chapter 9: Bees

5. Explain the relationship between the color of honey and its flavor.

   _____
   _____
   _____

6. In what medicinal way can honey be useful?

   _____
   _____
   _____

7. Honeybees gather nectar from about two thousand flowers in order to make a pound of honey. Is this statement true or false?

   _____

After reading this selection, are you likely to try using honey in any new ways? Explain.

_____
_____
_____
_____

Spectrum Reading Grade 8

Name _____

Chapter 9: Bees

> How does a summer away from home change Catalina forever?

Summer of the Bees

Catalina stood in the open doorway at the back of the shop and stared across the wide green field of clover. At the farthest end of the field were the stacked beehives, looking like a line of sugar cubes running along the edge of the woods. The white hives were slightly blurry, but Catalina knew by now that it was clouds of bees swarming that made the hives look fuzzy, and not simply the distance. She sighed and turned to head back into the shop, hardly believing that the summer was already over.

In the front room, Aunt Josefina was rearranging a display of beeswax candles and honey-scented soaps. She looked up as Catalina came in and then frowned at the expression on her niece's face. "Oh, sweetheart," she said, "you look so sad. We've had such a beautiful summer working together, and you've been such an enormous help. Besides, your family missed you terribly, and they can't wait to see you."

Catalina nodded and managed a small smile, but she could feel the tears trying to escape from her eyes. Aunt Josefina was right; it had been a great summer. In fact, it had been the most fantastic summer of Catalina's life, and it couldn't have come at a better time. Catalina was incredibly surprised when her parents suggested an idea: Catalina would spend two months in the country with her aunt Josefina.

Catalina's parents had driven her three hours north to the little town where her aunt lived, and she had spent the summer helping run Josefina's Candle Shop. Aunt Josefina kept her own bees—thousands of them—and she gathered the honey and beeswax to make candles, soaps, lotions, candies, and other products she sold in the shop. Catalina learned how to make candles, use molds to make soaps, run the cash register, wrap gifts, and package up goods to be shipped all over the country. She had even gotten to dress in the beekeeper's outfit and gather the honey herself.

When she wasn't working, she had explored some of the other stores in town and befriended a couple of the other shopkeepers. She also loved exploring the trails through the woods circling the clover field behind the shop. It really had been a perfect summer—and now it was over.

Name _____

Chapter 9: Bees

Catalina knew she had changed. Aunt Josefina had treated her like an adult for much of their time together. They had worked side-by-side, like two grown-up friends chatting away as they completed the day's chores. Catalina had even managed the shop by herself a few times when her aunt needed to run errands. Her self-esteem grew all summer, and now she would head into high school with newfound confidence.

The little bell hanging on the shop's front door jangled, announcing a customer coming in, but when Catalina looked over to the entrance, it was her mom and dad who stood there smiling. Behind them, her brother, Luiz, held the hand of her baby sister, Valeria. Catalina stared in amazement: Valeria was walking!

Catalina ran over and hugged each of them. She suddenly realized that as great as the summer had been, she was ready to go home.

Her mom said, "Goodness, Cat! You look like you grew a foot taller!"

"Nah, I just feel like I did," Catalina replied, "and I guess it shows."

Spectrum Reading Grade 8

Name _____

Chapter 9: Bees

Answer the questions about *Summer of the Bees*.

1. What idea did Catalina's parents have?

   _____

   _____

2. Catalina is sad that the summer is over, but by the end of the story, she is ready to go home. Why?

   _____

   _____

   _____

3. Which of the following statements best describes the story's theme? Place a check mark on the line of the best answer.

   _____ Hard work and a sense of responsibility can help build self-confidence.

   _____ Before others can help you, you must first help yourself.

   _____ Hard work is its own reward.

4. Complete the sentence below to identify the simile in the first paragraph.

   _____ are compared to

   _____ .

Name _____

Chapter 9: Bees

5. Personification is when an object or animal is described with human characteristics. Identify the example of personification in paragraph 3.

_____

_____

_____

6. How did being in charge of the store affect Catalina? Use evidence from the text to support your answer.

_____

_____

_____

> Who are the adult friends in your life? What are the benefits of these friendships compared to friendships with your peers?
>
> _____
>
> _____
>
> _____
>
> _____
>
> _____
>
> _____

Spectrum Reading Grade 8

Chapter 9: Bees

> What is it like to be a bee?

Morning Song of the Bees
by Louisa May Alcott

"Awake! awake! for the earliest gleam
Of golden sunlight shines
On the rippling waves, that brightly flow
Beneath the flowering vines.
Awake! awake! for the low, sweet chant
Of the wild-birds' morning hymn
Comes floating by on the fragrant air,
Through the forest cool and dim;
Then spread each wing,
And work, and sing,
Through the long, bright sunny hours;
O'er the pleasant earth
We journey forth,
For a day among the flowers.

"Awake! awake! for the summer wind
Hath bidden the blossoms unclose,
Hath opened the violet's soft blue eye,
And wakened the sleeping rose.
And lightly they wave on their slender stems
Fragrant, and fresh, and fair,
Waiting for us, as we singing come
To gather our honey-dew there.
Then spread each wing,
And work, and sing,
Through the long, bright sunny hours;
O'er the pleasant earth
We journey forth,
For a day among the flowers!"

Name _____

Chapter 9: Bees

> Answer the questions about "Morning Song of the Bees."

1. Who is the speaker of the poem? How do you know?

   _____

   _____

2. What is the mood of the poem? What words are a clue?

   _____

   _____

3. Which line of the poem do you think is the most important? Explain.

   _____

   _____

   _____

4. Draw a response to the poem. What do you "see" while reading the poem?

Spectrum Reading Grade 8

Chapter 9: Bees

What do bees know about math?

Brilliant Bees

A scientist in Australia, Dr. Scarlett Howard, is teaching math to honeybees. And her "students" are honeybees living in hives in a field near the Australian university where she works. Dr. Howard has learned that honeybees can add, subtract, and understand the concept of zero. How does she do this?

Howard teaches one bee at a time. The bee is placed inside a maze, which is a covered box in the shape of the letter Y. The bee enters at the bottom of the Y and sees a math problem (a card printed with several shapes in one of two colors). For example, blue shapes mean *add 1* and yellow shapes mean *subtract 1*. At the split of the Y, two answers await.

Name _____

Chapter 9: Bees

If the bee chooses the correct path, it is rewarded with a treat. Like with most animal training, Howard uses a reward system. The honeybees are rewarded with sugar water for correct answers and tonic water, which the bees find bitter, for incorrect answers.

To teach bees the concept of zero, Dr. Howard began teaching number relationships. Once a bee understood "less than," she tested it with a card that had zero shapes. Could a bee recognize that zero shapes is "less than" a small number of shapes? They sure could. Dr. Howard determined that bees must have a built-in understanding that zero is smaller than any positive integer.

Dr. Howard says that she can see the bees' decision-making in the way they fly and move. The bees go back to the hive to deliver some of the reward and to inform others in the hive where food is located using their scent. In this experiment, a bee marks the the correct answer. Dr. Howard cleans the cards so that the next bee does not "cheat."

Dr. Howard has some other assessments in mind, such as testing bees' response to negative numbers and their ability to count from left to right. Testing bees isn't like testing humans. A bee's motivation is different. There is much understanding that needs to happen before a question can be answered.

It is safe to say that Dr. Howard is just one of many zoologists helping us understand how intelligent other species can be. Now, that's some buzzworthy news to take back to the hive!

Spectrum Reading Grade 8

Name _____

Chapter 9: Bees

> Answer the questions about *Brilliant Bees*.

1. What is the author's opinion of Dr. Howard's work? Cite evidence from the selection to support your answer.

   _____

   _____

   _____

   _____

2. Describe how Dr. Howard "teaches" the bees.

   _____

   _____

   _____

   _____

3. How might Dr. Howard's research help other scientists?

   _____

   _____

   _____

   _____

Name _____

Chapter 9: Bees

4. Why do you think Dr. Howard designed a Y-shaped maze to test the bees? Cite evidence from the text to support your answer.

_____

_____

_____

_____

Dr. Howard's research shows that bees can learn. What other species of animal do you think would be interesting to teach? Why?

_____

_____

_____

_____

_____

_____

_____

_____

Spectrum Reading Grade 8

Answer Key

AWV: Answers will vary.
E: Answers to the Enrichment question

Chapter 1: Women in History

Stanton and Anthony, page 12
1. Stanton organized a convention to bring about awareness to the lack of women's rights in marriage, politics, etc.
2. All of the above
3. The reading selection focuses on a time after the Civil War and before the 19th amendment was ratified.
4. An abolitionist was a person who was against slavery and supported efforts and people who would end slavery.
5. The author thinks they were strong, determined women who worked well together for a common goal. The two made a great team that dominated the women's rights movement for more than 50 years.
6. AWV

Ella Fitzgerald, page 16
1. famous
2. AWV. Possible answer: The author included the text to show that Fitzgerald's confidence grew because of her natural talent.
3. 1, 4, 2, 3
4. The text says, Her talent and charm pleased a wide range of listeners around the world and helped make jazz a more popular genre.
5. AWV. Possible answer: She was one of the first women to popularize jazz and other genres.
E: AWV

Eleanor Roosevelt, page 19
1. the people who previously held a particular job
2. AWV: Possible answers: She held press conferences, traveled, lectured, and spoke on the radio.
3. Because Franklin was ill, Eleanor attended meetings and reported back to to Franklin. She saw and listened, giving the meaning to the phrase "eyes and ears"
4. This text is an example of a biography. Biographies are often written about a real person including facts about their life and their accomplishments.

Queen Liliuokalani, page 22
1. AWV, but should include an explanation connected to the text.
2. The word republic means a body of people who vote on their leaders.
3. 5, 3, 4, 2, 1
4. Some Americans were in favor of Hawaii being annexed because they had business interests in goods being shipped from Hawaii. If Hawaii became a state, Queen Liliuokalani would not have power over Hawaii's ports and business deals.
5. AWV. Possible answer: Queen Liuokalani was well-educated, well-traveled, and an advocate for her people. The second paragraph tells us about her education and her travels. The third paragraph tells how an outbreak of smallpox made the queen close the ports to protect her people.
E: AWV

Chapter 2: Ordinary Kids, Extraordinary Deeds

Kid of the Year, page 28
1. contaminated drinking water, cyberbullying, and opioid addiction
2. observe, brainstorm, research, build, communicate
3. AWV. Possible answer: Gitanjali wants to motivate teens to take charge of their future and make a change one small step at a time.
4. AWV. Possible answer: Gitanjali was on the cover of *Time* Magazine's December 14, 2020 issue.
5. AWV. Possible answer: . . . one of the most popular magazines in the country . . .
E: AWV. Check students' timelines

Spread Kindness Like Wildflowers, page 32
1. AWV. Possible answer: "Anything is possible with the power of belief, the power of kindness . . ."
2. Orion says that you can influence just one person, and that one person can influence someone in their own lives, causing a ripple effect.
3. AWV. Possible answer: for effect and imagery
4. AWV
5. AWV. Possible answer: Orion says being kind is one small act of kindness that can make a big difference.
E: AWV

Volunteering Is for Kids, page 35
1. A good way to start volunteering is to think about something you're interested in, good at, or touched by.
2. AWV
E: AWV

Answer Key

Chapter 3: Art & Illustration

Who Is Banksy?, page 40
1. AWV. Possible answers: anonymous, sneaky, clever
2. walls, bridges, war zones, etc.
3. AWV. Possible answer: Just as the art was sold, half of it was destroyed by a shredding machine Banksy had hidden in the frame.
4. AWV. Possible answer: Banksy does not believe art should be owned. It is for all to enjoy.
E. AWV

Alma Thomas, page 44
1. The author included that text because they felt it was an important part of her upbringing to show that Alma, herself, embraced those values too.
2. exhibition means to display; to show
3. Thomas decided she wanted to focus on happiness rather than the inhumanities of the time.
4. It is important to the text because it shows that she was a devoted teacher and it can take a lifetime to realize one's hard work and efforts.
5. The author wrote the selection to inform and inspire.
E: AWV

Anime for All Ages, page 48
1. They are flawed, but they strive for perfection, which relates to the pressure to succeed in Japanese education and culture.
2. In the years leading up to the war, the government wanted artists to show only positive aspects of Japan. After the war, there was more freedom, and artists could draw what they wanted to.
3. to inform the reader about Japanese anime and its history
4. made larger or greater than normal
5. Hair color gives the reader information about the character's personality.
6. F, F, T, T
E: AWV

Finding a Way to the Comic Convention, page 52
1. Shaun loves anything to do with space. Malik was slow to learn to read and developed an early love of animation and graphic novels.
2. pay back
3. AWV. Possible answer: They seem like friends. They want to help each other out and support each other.
4. AWV
5. Malik
6. Malik can go to a comic book convention if he can save enough for airfare, but he worries he'll never have enough money.
7. Shaun helps Malik figure out what he needs to do to save enough money. He also offers Malik half his allowance if Malik will do his chores.
E: AWV

Born to Draw, page 56
1. Aisha is frustrated because she plans to become wealthy as a comic illustrator and her parents are not supporting that goal.
2. She has a lot of free time over the summer to draw and develop comics; once school starts, her time will be more limited.
3. AWV. Possible answer: Aisha draws comic stories, and each scene in a comic is drawn in its own section. The storyboards are probably the different scenes of a comic.
4. AWV. Possible answer: Miss Santoro tells Aisha to be honest with her parents about how she feels.
5. AWV
6. AWV. Possible answer: Miss Santoro is a good teacher because she knows her students well enough to see if one of them is upset. She also takes the time to find out how she can help.
E: AWV

Chapter 4: Fossils

Stuck in the Pits, page 62
1. informational text
2. AWV. Possible answer: No, it's not likely because the fossils found there are of animals that lived about 50,000 years ago, while dinosaurs lived 65 million years ago.
3. dire wolf
4. AWV. Possible answers: Cause: Small animals would become trapped in the tar pits. Effect: Larger animals would come feed on them and become trapped too.
5. Project 23 involves fossil remains that were found when a new parking garage was being built. There are 23 boxes that the scientists need to sort through, identify, and catalog.
6. This statement is true because new chemical and excavation techniques have been developed.
7. AWV

Fossil Hunters, page 66
1. AWV. Possible answer: Experts may be able to learn more about your find based on its location, the rocks around it, etc.
2. biology, geology
3. AWV. Possible answer: These are the places where layers of rock are exposed, so you may be able to see fossils that otherwise would be hidden.
4. This statement is false because they also spend a lot of time in offices and laboratories to analyze and study the discoveries they make.
5. In paragraph 3, the author states that paleontology can be exciting work because you can find a new creature or a missing piece in a mystery scientists have been trying to solve. The author states that paleontology can be painstaking work because you dig for long periods of time with few finds and recovering a fossil is often slow.
6. doing a puzzle
7. AWV. Possible answer: If a scientist is familiar with the biology and anatomy of other animals, that knowledge can help them figure out how to assemble a skeleton.
E: AWV

Spectrum Reading Grade 8

Answer Key

Working with History, page 70
1. AWV. Possible answers: She sighs at the red light. She eagerly hops out of the car.
2. AWV. Possible answers: It reminds her of her grandpa. She loves how quiet it is. She loves looking at the displays and exhibits.
3. AWV. Possible answer: someone who does a lot of different jobs or knows how to do many things
4. AWV. Possible answer: Yes, because she loves the museum and seems excited about her new job. She is looking forward to doing the tasks taht Mr. Rockwell describes.
5. lay of the land; It means to show someone all of the places and spaces of a certain location.
E: AWV

Sue Hendrickson, page 74
1. adventurous; Sue went on many dives and digs and adventures throughout her life and career.
2. 1, 3, 4, 2, 5
3. AWV but may include that the scientist knew of her work as a successful diver and fossil extractor.
4. She was observing the land around her in South Dakota while waiting for her team to return to their vehicle.
E: AWV

Coming Back to Life, page 78
1. AWV. Possible answer: De-extinction involves using the DNA of an extinct animals to recreate the species.
2. the last living Pyrenean ibex
3. They lived too long ago, so there are no samples of DNA to use in trying to recreate them.
4. AWV. Possible answer: They feel that there are thousands of living species of plants and animals that are in need of protection. They believe that human resources would be better spent in locating, studying, and preserving these living animals than in trying to bring back ones that no longer exist.
5. AWV. Possible answer: Scientist hope to be able to recreate a woolly mammoth one day using the frozen samples of mammoth hair, tissue, and skin they found.
E: AWV

An Ancient Memento, page 82
1. awe and respect
2. AWV. Possible answer: While Sierra is volunteering at the natural history museum, she drops a fossil. She has to take responsibility for it and tell her supervisor.
3. fake
4. Sierra
5. She's embarrassed and worries about whether she'll lose her job.
6. sympathetic
E: AWV

Chapter 5: Search and Rescue

Hidden Danger, page 88
1. an avalanche and the way accumulated snow slides down the windshield when it gets warmer inside the car
2. AWV. Possible answer: The analogy gives me something concrete and familiar to picture, which makes it easier to understand how an avalanche works
3. snow, a sloped surface, a trigger
4. Snowpack refers to layers of accumulated snow.
5. An avalanche is more likely to occur on open terrain, because there are no trees to help buffer the snow and keep it anchored.
6. The author just presents the facts.
7. Snow crystals that do not create a strong bond can create a weak layer, as can dramatic changes in temperature.
E: AWV

An Avalanche for Breakfast, page 92
1. The story does not explain.
2. The author's main purposes for writing this story are to entertain and to inform
3. The ski patrol looks for potential avalanche sites. Then, they use explosives to trigger the avalanche in a controlled environment.
4. the author's
5. Cause: The ski patrol locates the place where a person might be buried in the snow; Effect: Santiago yelled, "Egg-valanche!"; Cause: Santiago had an incorrect idea about what an avalanche is.
6. If they are trapped in snow, the radio transmitter will tell where they are.
7. If people are buried in the snow during the avalanche, the dogs use their sense of smell to locate them. Then, the dogs lead the ski patrol members back to where the people are buried.

Canine Rescue, page 96
1. recorded; proven
2. AWV. Possible answer: It let them know that they are probably going to a rescue.
3. AWV. Possible answers: Fact: Within minutes, Aspen began digging rapidly. Opinion: It doesn't surprise me at all that Aspen is a hero!
4. Dogs can detect human scent more quickly than humans can. They can search more quickly than humans too.
5. AWV. Possible answer: areas under the snow where a human's scent has accumulated or pooled
6. courageous, dependable, athletic, energetic, studious
7. Possible answers: Elizabeth and Mitchell are missing their own dogs. They run over to see the rescue dogs. They can't wait to see the dogs after the rescue.
8. The climax of the story is when the skiers get trapped by the avalanche.
9. Aspen finds the spot where one of the skiers was buried, and both skiers were rescued.

188   Spectrum Reading **Grade 8**

Answer Key

Chapter 6: Let's Eat

Julia Child, page 102
1. biography
2. AWV. Possible answer: The author organized the information chronologically, or in time order. This was a good choice because the text is a biography, and people live their lives in time order. It makes sense to retell the events in a person's life in time order.
3. AWV. Possible answer: Julia Child was born in America, but she spent a lot of time in France and learned how to become a great French chef. Then, along with two other women, she wrote and published a book about French cooking that became a bestseller in the United States, and she hosted a cooking show called The French Chef.
4. The book was so big, some publishers thought it was too much like an encyclopedia.
5. Julia Child's first television show was called The French Chef.
E: AWV

Julia's Famous French Bread, page 106
1. to explain to the reader
2. AWV. Possible answer: The author's purpose is to explain the steps needed to bake bread. Organizing the steps by number helps make it clear when each step needs to be completed.
3. AWV. Possible answer: The ingredients are listed first so the cook can gather them and have them ready before beginning any of the steps.
4. 7 hours
5. Slash the loaves diagonally.
6. AWV, but probably pretty difficult given the time and number of steps involved.
E: AWV

Garden Veggie Frittata, page 110
1. to draw the readers attention to this important reminder
2. salt and pepper
3. cook in a pan
4. decorate
5. The eggs should be starting to become firm.
6. 3, 2, 1, 6, 5, 4
E: AWV

An Experimental Appetite, page 114
1. O, F, O, F
2. Alex is more adventurous than Emily is about trying new foods.
3. He loves to try new foods and likes fish.
4. a thin sheet of seaweed
5. It would make it seem like Alex was afraid instead of excited.
6. Alex and Emily both enjoy the sushi and want to find more restaurants to try new cuisines.
E: AWV

Chapter 7: Space

Planting a Seed for the Future, page 120
1. Jessica's hypothesis is that foxglove will grow more quickly in a reduced-gravity envirnoment.
2. At the beginning of the story, Jessica was excited but didn't think she would have a chance of designing an experiement in time. By the end of the story, she felt proud and confident that her experiment had a chance of winning the contest.
3. Her mother grows it, and it is used in treating heart patients.
4. Jessica has made a play on words. A *seed* of thought is the beginning of an idea, and her experiment will use plant *seeds*.
5. Jessica's experiment requires an atmosphere of reduced gravity, so space is an ideal place to test it.
6. AWV. Possible answers: Propel action: "Did you see this?" asked Jessica."What an awesome opportunity!" (Jessica looks at the details of the contest that the poster was publicizing. One lucky student would have his or her experiment performed in space.) Reveal character: The text reveals that Jessica is thorough and studious. It says: "She grabbed a dictionary off the shelf. Words like atrial, fibrillation, and cardiac were coming up regularly in her research, which was a little intimidating, and she wanted to be able to use them correctly as she developed her experiment." Provoke decisions: The text says: "Despite being a toxic plant, foxglove was obviously valuable to heart patients and Jessica thought that finding more efficient ways to grow the plant might reduce the price of the medication produced from it."

Curiosity in Space, page 124
1. F, T, T, F
2. Research indicated that the crater was most likely filled in with sediment that was carried into it by flowing water. Proving that water existed on Mars was one of *Curiosity*'s main missions.
3. flying to different areas of the Martian landscape
4. AWV. Possible answers: One advantage is that materials can be analyzed on Mars and do not need to be sent back to Earth. One disadvantage is if that something goes wrong with the lab, it cannot be repaired.
5. AWV. Possible answer: *Microbial* means something very small that can be seen only with a microscope.
E: AWV

Spectrum Reading **Grade 8**

Answer Key

Out of This World Experience, page 128
1. You should study whatever field you most enjoy because then you will be passionate about your work. Astronauts often have varied backgrounds in the sciences.
2. Ms. Farrow
3. AWV. Possible answer: It tells the reader that Ms. Farrow is thoughtful. She is also proud of the work she does and humans' progress in learning about the universe.
4. NASA has to carefully screen astronauts for health issues because of limited access to treatment in space.
5. AWV
6. AWV. Possible answer: The universe is so big it seems unlikely that only Earth could support life. Maybe she thinks it would be arrogant because it implies that humans are so special that there could be nothing else like us.
E. AWV

Moon Veggies, page 132
1. fresh fruits and vegetables
2. AWV. Possible answer: They would not have a chance of surviving in the moon's harsh atmosphere.
3. AWV. Possible answer: Plants and humans need many of the same things to live. If plants can survive, humans might one day have a chance of living there too. Also, the plants can provide food for humans living on the moon.
4. They can remind people of home and the atmosphere on Earth.
5. inform
6. nutrient-rich paper, air, and water
7. Explorers living in a simulated Mars habitat missed fruits and vegetables more than any other food.
E: AWV

Home, Home on the Moon, page 136
1. Markus, his sister, and his father are traveling to a colony on the Moon to be with their mother. Markus does not want to make the move, and he already misses Earth terribly. After arriving at the colony, Markus is surprised and happy to run into an old classmate who has lived at the colony for a while and will show him around.
2. AWV. Possible answers: Families travelling in space. People living on the moon.
3. AWV. Possible answers: A family moving to a new place. Markus's feelings about leaving the home he knew best.
4. The author used the simile to help the reader visualize how bright Earth looked.
5. For most of the story, Markus is very unhappy about the move. The author uses words and phrases such as: *grim, desolate, leaving Earth was tough, breaking down into tears, emptiness of space, lifeless,* and so on.
6. Markus is relieved to find someone he knows already living at the colony. The author shows how he feels by writing the words *Markus smiled.*
7. a mall
E: AWV

Chapter 8: Under Water

The Sturgeon General, page 142
1. everlasting
2. awareness
3. AWV. Possible answers: curious, adventurous, intelligent
4. Oceanographer Sylvia Earle has had a lifelong fascination with and dedication to the world's oceans and is working to protect them for future generations.
5. biography
6. sperm whales
7. The blue heart refers to Earth's oceans, and Earle believes we need to keep them healthy in order to keep our planet alive and healthy.

Fishing for Change, page 146
1. In Europe, it is very popular, but in America it has been regarded as a "garbage fish" in the past.
2. AWV
3. AWV. Possible answer: They are close and enjoying spending time together.
4. Most people find the name *dogfish* to be unappealing.
5. true
6. The demand for dogfish has gone up, therefore this makes the price of the dogfish go up. Typically when something is in demand, the price of it goes up.
7. optimistic
E: AWV

Going the Distance, page 150
1. AWV. Possible answer: Both are long distance events, and they both require the athletes to have built up a great deal of endurance.
2. It keeps his body from chafing, keeps him warmer, and wards off jellyfish stings.
3. AWV. Possible answers: athletic, determined, friendly
4. jellyfish
5. informing the reader about long-distance swimming
6. AWV
E: AWV

Find a Way, page 154
1. AWV. Possible answers: strong currents, throwing her off course, an asthma attack, and jellyfish stings
2. Cuba, Florida
3. AWV. Possible answer: The waves kept tossing her against the cage during her first attempt. She might not have liked the feeling of being caged.
4. Possible answer: She wanted people to know that they can follow their dreams and they are never too old to try to reach their goals.
5. Possible answers: persistent, brave, determined
6. Her team used an electronic shark repellant. She used a nylon body suit, a mask, gloves, and booties to protext herself from jellyfish stings.
7. AWV
E: AWV

Answer Key

The Age of Aquarius, page 158
1. mission, ecosystems, decrease
2. the difference in pressure deep underwater and at the surface
3. Florida
4. AWV. Possible answer: They can closely observe the reef and its in habitants over time. They can assess the damages of pollution and determine ways to protect the reef.
E: AWV

Every Lap Counts, page 162
1. to help a fellow student who is ill and cannot afford medical care
2. 10
3. Possible answer: Dylan is a generous, caring friend and has strong willpower to keep himself going.
4. competitiveness
5. Dylan's
6. AWV. Possible answer: If the story were told from Charley's perspective, there would not be descriptions of swimming. The author might describe how he feels sitting on the bench, as well as how the illness is making him feel. We would hear Charley's thoughts instead of Dylan's.
7. hearing: the way water affects the sounds of the crowd; feeling: burning muscles; sight: Kaitlyn splashing; red letters on banner
E: AWV

The Ocean, page 165
1. The message of the poem is that the ocean can be a dangerous place.
2. The mood is dark and serious.
3. The author develops the mood through word choice and imagery. Some words that point to this are: fury, awful, weep, graves, etc.
4. AWV. Possible answers should include swapping out dark and serious words with light and happy words.

Chapter 9: Bees

Honey Hill Farm, page 170
1. AWV, but could include the following:

Type	Pro	Con
Langstroth Hive	Easy access to bees	Boxes are bulky to store and heavy to lift
Top Bar Hive	Less disruptive to bees	Proper ventilation can be a problem

2. calm the bees
3. AWV, but could include that Mr. Loughton is a fair and honest teacher. He doesn't insert his opinion, but provides the lessons he's learned and let's others decide for themselves.
4. AWV, but could include, that yes, they are getting a first-hand look at what beekeeping requires.
5. The Langstroth hive because it is better insulated than a top bar hive.
6. The author's purposes for writing this selection are to inform and show how text can capture multiple viewpoints allowing for fair comparison.
E: AWV

Sweet as Honey, page 174
1. AWV. Possible answer: The author is enthusiastic about honey. They use phrases like "if you're lucky," "it's a miracle of sorts," and "it's one of the most perfect foods on the planet."
2. You can blend together honey and olive oil to make a conditioner.
3. insect
4. AWV: Possible answer: It was used as a gift to the gods and as an element of embalming fluid for mummies.
5. Lighter honeys tend to have a milder flavor, and darker honeys have a stronger flavor.
6. It can soothe a sore throat or calm a cough.
7. false
E: AWV

Answer Key

Summer of the Bees, page 178
1. Catalina's parents suggested Catalina spend two months in the country with her aunt Josephina.
2. When Catalina sees her family, she realizes how much she misses them and is ready to go home.
3. Hard work and a sense of responsibility can help build self-confidence.
4. Beehives, sugar cubes
5. Tears are described as trying to escape Catalina's eyes.
6. AWV. Possible answer: Catalina liked being in charge of the store because she felt like an adult. She says that her self-esteem grew all summer, and now she would head into high school with newfound confidence.
E: AWV

Morning Song of the Bees, page 181
1. The speaker of the poem is the bees. The author uses first-person pronouns like *we* and *our*.
2. excited; The words, "Awake, awake" repeated over and over signal that there is excitement.
3. AWV
E: AWV

Brilliant Bees, page 184
1. AWV, but could include that the author likes Dr. Howard's work. The sentence, It is safe to say that Dr. Howard is just one of many zoologists helping us understand how intelligent other species can be shows the author's opinion.
2. Dr. Howard uses a maze and reward system to teach the bees.
3. AWV, but may include that Dr. Howard's methods for testing and teaching bees can be applied to other species.
4. AWV. Possible answer: The maze has one entrance and then has only two arms for two answers.
E: AWV

PHOTO CREDITS: page 10: ©Everett Collection/Shutterstock; page 11: ©Everett Collection/Shutterstock; page 14: ©Universal Images Group/Newscom; page 18: ©World History Archive/Newscom; page 20: ©LoC/Underwood Archives/Universal Images Group/Newscom; page 27: ©Luiz Rampelotto/EuropaNewswire/picture alliance/Luiz Rampelot/Newscom; page 31: ©Everett Collection/Newscom; page 39: ©Peter Harvie/Alamy Stock Photo; page 42: ©NB/DeptComm/Alamy Stock Photo; page 43: ©wavebreakmedia/Shutterstock; page 72: ©Przemek Klos/Shutterstock; page 73: ©Miss Ostrich/Shutterstock; page 87: ©Richard Nantais/Shutterstock; page 100: ©Rick Friedman/Polaris/Newscom; page 109: ©Brent Hofacker/Shutterstock; page 123: ©Triff/Shutterstock; page 131: ©eurobanks/Shutterstock; page 153: ©Nancy Kaszerman/ZUMA Press/Newscom; page 157: ; page 169: ©Terelyuk/Shutterstock; page 173: ©Barnuti Daniel Ioan/Shutterstock; page 182: ©Bryan_Tunche/Shutterstock; page 183: ©Butler Stock Photography/Shutterstock